The Texas Constitution:

The People, History, and Government of the Lone Star State

The Texas Constitution:

The People, History, and Government of the Lone Star State

Terri B. Davis
and
James P. Nelson

LITERARY PRESS
LAMAR UNIVERSITY

ISBN: 978-1-942956-48-8
Library of Congress Control Number: 2017962751

Book design: Theresa Ener

Lamar University Literary Press
Beaumont, Texas

Acknowledgments

We would like to thank our colleagues and friends for assisting us in the editing and review of the textbook. Boyd Lanier, Associate Professor of Political Science, Lamar University, provided invaluable service in the editing of the textbook. Content reviewers gave the authors valuable and thoughtful feedback on the content and readability of the chapters: Craig Tahaney, attorney and Instructor of Political Science, Lamar University; Sara Gubala, Instructor of Political Science, Lamar University; Mary Ann Palmer, attorney; and Daye Dunn Collins, historian. Jacob Rost and Sarah Rost, to whom this textbook is dedicated, reviewed the chapters through the eyes of undergraduate students and gave us a fresh perspective on the subjects covered in the textbook. We are especially grateful to Theresa Ener for providing countless hours of editing and the professional expertise in converting the manuscript into digital and print format; Dr. Jerry Craven, Editor of Lamar University Literary Press; and Dr. Jim Sanderson for making our "idea" a reality. Our sincere thanks to everyone who contributed to the final product.

Recent Nonfiction from Lamar University Press

Jean Andrews, *High Tides, Low Tides*
Robert Murray Davis, *Levels of Incompetence: An Academic Life*
Ted L. Estess, *Fishing Spirit Lake*
William Guest, *Places You Want to Go*
Dominique Inge, *A Garden on the Brazos*
Terry C. Maxwell, *Tales of a Journeyman Naturalist*
Jim McJunkin, *Deep Sleep*
Jeanetta Calhoun Mish, *Oklahomeland*
Jim Sanderson, *Sanderson's Fiction Writing Manual*
Steven Schroeder, *What's Love Got to Do With It? A city out of thin air*

For Information on these and other books, go to
www.lamar.edu/literarypress

This textbook is dedicated to Jacob Samuel Rost and Sarah Renee Rost.

CONTENTS

Introduction
by Terri B. Davis

Welcome to a study of the Texas Constitution. My motivation for writing a textbook on the Texas Constitution and state government was three-fold. First, state politics can change rapidly and university students must spend a great deal of money on textbooks only to find the texts are outdated almost as soon as they are purchased. Having worked full-time to support my undergraduate and most of my graduate education, this textbook *allows students an opportunity to read and learn about the Texas Constitution through a digitally formatted text offered free of charge to students and instructors.*

Second, I am a native Texan and self-proclaimed "blue-collar scholar" who appreciates the value of hard work and a story well-told. Some students attending Texas universities (particularly online students) are non-Texas residents that have expressed dislike for the state's requirement that all students in Texas colleges and universities must learn about the state's Constitution and government before they can earn their degrees. Other students are native Texans and have voiced discontent with some existing Texas government textbooks that present the state's history, constitutions, and government in a dry, bland fashion that is inconsistent with the state's vibrant, remarkable, and often exciting political culture. Dr. Nelson and I have addressed such concerns by attempting *to tell the story of Texas government through the voice of native Texans writing for an audience that includes both Texas- and non-Texas residents.* Regardless of your current geographic location, learning about Texas government can be intellectually stimulating, spark critical thinking, and compel reflection about one's own political narrative. We have learned a great deal about Texas (and ourselves) while researching and writing the text and hope you do as well.

Finally, a primary feature of Texas political culture is a strong belief in limited government. Simply stated, Texans tend to resent government—any government—"telling them what to do." We didn't like it under Spanish colonial rule; we didn't like it during the period of Reconstruction; and we don't like it now. But, implicit in the social contract that creates representative democracies is an understanding

13

that citizens will abide by the decisions made by their elected representatives. As mentioned above, the Texas legislature has mandated that all college and university undergraduate students take two American government core curriculum courses in order to receive their degrees, and one of those courses must contain a Texas Constitution component. Furthermore, the Texas Higher Education Coordinating Board has mandated that all core curriculum courses (including American Government I and II) contain specific core objectives including critical thinking skills, communication skills, and social and personal responsibility. And, the Southern Association of Colleges and Schools (SACS) requires all accredited universities to provide students with courses and materials that satisfy "best practices" and well-articulated student learning outcomes. We have sought *to write a textbook that allows instructors and the courses they design to meet if not exceed state and accreditation agency requirements while simultaneously allowing students expanded opportunities for intellectual exploration, reflection, and insight.* The textbook is also designed to allow higher education government *teachers a high degree of professional autonomy to teach and construct their courses consistent with their own education, training, and pedagogical style, and to give them a fair chance to do what they do best: educate students and citizens about the national and state constitutions that together create the American federal system of government.*

Another part of our mission is to tell a story of the Texas Constitution of 1876 that includes at least some of the narratives of Texans that have traditionally been overlooked in government textbooks. To achieve this mission, each chapter contains blocked and highlighted sections containing stories about people that helped shape the history, various constitutions, and governments of the state. Women, for example, played and continue to play a large role in shaping Texas government and politics. But, as a group, women did not easily fit into any of the sections and subsections of the textbook since they are members of many demographic groups (race, ethnicity, national origin, etc.). For this reason, an ongoing series, "The Wild and Wonderful Women of Texas," provides information about important but little-known women in Texas history. The women featured exhibit fierce individualism and the fighting spirit that many Texans—and Texas political culture in general—are known for. Another ongoing

14

series, "For the Record," seeks to clarify certain misconceptions some students may hold about specific events in Texas history and the structure of Texas government, or to provide additional information about subjects touched on but not elaborated on in the main body of the textbook. I have also tried to provide the names of present-day cities, towns, and areas where historic events occurred so that "road trip historians" such as myself will have a reference point from which to stop and explore some of the more than 16,000 state historical markers[1] during their travels throughout this vast state.

Our first "For the Record" contains a brief introduction of the textbook's first author. A similar entry about the second author follows. As you peruse the introduction, you are encouraged to reflect on your own personal history, ancestry, and experiences as they relate to Texas history and government. Instructors may—or may not—choose to write their own brief introductions, and allow students to write their brief personal histories in their on-campus and online classes as a way for students and instructors to get to know one another and share their Texas experiences.

For the Record: About the Author, Terri B. Davis

Terri Burney Davis was born in Hopkins County, Texas. Her Texas roots may be traced back at least five generations. She is a descendent of the families Bryan (immigrants from County Cork, Ireland, eventually settling in Kaufman County), Porter (primarily British, migrating from the Trans-Appalachian south and settling in Collin County), and Burney (Scotch-Irish, with reported Texas settlement in Tarrant County). Some members of these families migrated separately to Hopkins County around the turn of the twentieth century and came to settle in Sulphur Springs.

Davis moved from Sulphur Springs to Tyler in 1981 to pursue a career as a paralegal and attend night school. She worked full-time and graduated with honors from the University of Texas at Tyler with a bachelor degree in Political Science (1987) and a master degree in Interdisciplinary Studies (1989). Study abroad opportunities allowed her to spend a summer in Costa Rica and several weeks in China—experiences that, combined with higher education, gave Davis the confidence to apply to the doctoral program at the University of Texas at Austin. She was accepted at the University of Texas, placed on a 'master teacher' track, and quickly assigned her own class of over 500 students. In 1994, she joined the faculty at Baylor University, where she taught courses in American constitutional law, government, and political theory while finishing her Ph.D. dissertation in United States constitutional theory and history under the direction of Professor Jeffrey K. Tulis.

Davis joined the faculty of Lamar University in 1996. She specializes in American constitutional and administrative law. She became Chair and Associate Professor of the Department of Political Science in 2010. Davis has won numerous teaching awards, and her research appears in peer-reviewed journals including *Studies in Media and Communication, Open Journal of Political Science, Comparative Sociology, Social Issues in America*, and *Law and Politics Book Review*.

For the Record: About the Author, James P. Nelson

James P. Nelson is originally from Baytown, Texas. He received his undergraduate education at Lee College (2002, A.S. Business Administration and Management) and Lamar University (2004, B.S. Political Science), and earned his Ph.D. in political science from The Florida State University (2011).

Nelson's first full-time academic job was at the University of Texas–Pan American (now University of Texas–Rio Grande Valley), where he taught courses while completing his doctoral dissertation. He was subsequently hired by Lamar University in Fall 2011. Nelson is currently Assistant Professor of Political Science at Lamar University. His research emphasizes political behavior in addition to sub-national U.S. politics. He has authored/co-authored multiple studies of state political policy as well. His research has been published in multiple peer-reviewed journals, and he looks forward to sharing his expertise on state government with readers of this text.

Unit 1: Early Texas History; Migration and Immigration; and the Constitutions, Political Culture, and People of Texas

Unit 1 provides the foundations for understanding the current Texas Constitution and state government and politics. It examines the early explorations, settlements, and disputes over Texas land; migration and immigration to the state; and the state's constitutions, political culture, and major participants that have impacted Texas government.

Chapter 1

Early Explorations, Settlements, and Disputes over Texas Land (1519–1836)

Chapter 1 discusses early Texas history. It focuses on various explorations, treaties, and agreements concerning Texas land and attempts by a number of individuals to liberate Texas from Spanish rule. Upon completing the chapter, you should be able to demonstrate knowledge about:

- ▸ Early Spanish and French explorations of Texas
- ▸ The names of key individuals and the contributions they made to early Texas history
- ▸ Treaties and agreements entered into concerning Texas land
- ▸ Attempts to liberate Texas from Spanish rule
- ▸ The importance of Austin's Colony

Spain, France, and Early Exploration and Settlement of Texas

The history of Texas is a very long one with human settlements tracing back at least 11,000 years before the arrival of Europeans. By the time the first European, ALONSO ALVAREZ DE PINEDA of Spain, arrived in present-day Texas in 1519 and explored and mapped the Texas coastline, Native American populations had long occupied lands from the Texas Gulf Coast to the Panhandle, and from the Piney Woods of East Texas to the barren plains of the south and west. Native American tribes such as the Karankawa, Caddo, Apache, Comanche, Wichita, Coahuiltecan, Neches, Tonkawa, and many others had established themselves as hunters, food gatherers, traders, artisans, and healers.[2]

Pineda's exploration of the Texas Gulf Coast was followed in

1528 by Cabeza de Vaca. After becoming shipwrecked on a sandbar off present-day Galveston Island, De Vaca's exploration team including ESTEBAN (also referred to in historical accounts as "Estevanico"), the first known African to arrive in Texas, was promptly enslaved by the native people of the area, the Karankawa Indians. Esteban's rudimentary medical knowledge and gift for languages increased his influence over the Karankawa, and after eight years he was released and set off to Mexico City to find *Cibolo*, the "Seven Cities of Gold."[3] De Vaca's exploration team was followed by Francisco Coronado, who from 1540 to 1542 led an expedition across Mexico into what is now northern Texas. Coronado's expedition mapped northern Texas, and for a time the explorer resided in Palo Duro Canyon near present-day Amarillo and Canyon.[4]

The 17th and 18th centuries were an era of both Spanish and French exploration of Texas. France laid claim to Texas with the settlement of present-day Matagorda Bay by La Salle in 1685,[5] and further explorations were made by St. Denis, who in the early 1700s made expeditions up the Red River, and La Harpe, who in 1718 established a trading post among the Caddo Indians in present-day Red River County.

The Wild and Wonderful Women of Texas: "Angelina" (birth unknown; death unknown)

"ANGELINA," the Christian name given at baptism to a Native American woman, was educated by Spanish friars at the Mission of San Juan Bautista on the Rio Grande River. She spoke Spanish as well as several Indian languages, and served as a translator for Luis Juchereau de St. Denis during his travels in East Texas. In 1718 and 1719, Angelina served as translator for an expedition that founded the Alamo and the city of San Antonio de Bexar. She is the only woman to have a Texas river, county, and national forest named for her.[6]

In response to increasing French activity and incursion, the Spanish viceroy in Mexico City prepared to establish colonies in Texas. The first official Spanish settlements were established in 1716 (present-day Nacogdoches); 1718 (present-day San Antonio); and 1721 (La Bahia near present-day Goliad).[7] Colonization by Spanish explorers and missionaries continued throughout the 1740s and 1750s to include both banks of the Rio Grande River in the areas surrounding present-day Laredo.[8] Although France officially abandoned its claims to Texas in 1762 with the signing of the Treaty of Fontainebleau, settlement attempts continued to be made by French individuals such as the pirate Jean Lafitte, who in 1817 set up a "republic" on Galveston Island as a base from which to conduct smuggling and privateering activities; and the Napoleonic exiled General Charles Lallemand, who in 1818 established a settlement on the Trinity River near present-day Liberty.

For the Record: Jean Lafitte (1780?–1825?)

JEAN LAFITTE was born in Bayonne, France, to a French father and a Spanish mother. The family migrated from France to the island of Hispaniola, but then fled during a rebellion on the island. Jean and his brother, Pierre, arrived in New Orleans around 1804, and by 1808 were heavily involved in the smuggling trade. The brothers held shares in many privateers that sailed the Gulf and the Caribbean, and the privateers brought their prizes to the Lafitte brothers at Barataria, a village on the outskirts of New Orleans in present-day Jefferson Parish.[9]

The British asked Lafitte for his help during the War of 1812, but he rejected the offer and sided with the United States in hopes of gaining a pardon for his illegal activities. He supplied the United States with men, weapons, and his knowledge of the region, to help secure Andrew Jackson an overwhelming victory at the Battle of New Orleans (1814–1815).[10] Lafitte was not the only "scallywag" involved in Jackson's war. Using court records, vessel registries, and letters of marque, the National Archives at Atlanta recently documented over 200 cases of privateering and its accompanying "prizes of war" during the War of 1812.[11]

Schemers in New Orleans led by Louis Michel Aury sought to open a port on the Texas coast that would serve as a haven for privateers and a base for an attack against Texas. Aury arrived in

Galveston in July 1816 and was joined by the Mexican rebel José Manuel de Herrera on a mission to constitute Galveston as a *puerto habilitado* of the Mexican republic. In the meantime, Jean Lafitte was sent to Galveston as an agent in the Spanish secret service. There, Lafitte organized a government for Galveston and swore its allegiance to Mexico. In a plot to capture Aury, Lafitte's brother succeeded in causing so many of Aury's men to desert that Aury left the island. Lafitte secured the island republic in September 1817 and made it a center for smuggling and privateering.

The brothers made quite a team, with the more adventurous and conniving Jean handling the matters of their privateering business and the more capable Pierre managing intrigues with Spanish officials and the brothers' business arrangements in New Orleans. After almost three years of running the "Pirate Republic" of Galveston, it became clear to the Lafitte brothers that Spain would no longer support them and that the United States was determined to end their Galveston establishment. The Lafittes abandoned Galveston in May 1820 and sailed to Isla Mujeres, off the coast of Yucatán. There, Jean continued his illegal activities. He died around 1825.[12]

The Treaty of Fontainebleau (1762), the Louisiana Purchase (1803), and Disputes over Texas Land

The TREATY OF FONTAINEBLEAU is rarely discussed in Texas government textbooks but deserves mention because of its impact on later political and historical events in Texas history. First, the treaty was signed after Great Britain defeated France in the Seven Years' War. The treaty ceded to Spain all territory west of the Mississippi River including the "Isle of Orleans" (New Orleans). While Spain was not a direct participant in the Seven Years' War, Great Britain's gift to Spain was an attempt to strengthen ties and develop an alliance with Spain against France.[13] But, in the three decades following the signing of the treaty, the French military leader Napoleon Bonaparte took hold of Europe, and Spain again renewed its alliance with France. The two countries entered into a series of treaties that included Spain returning Louisiana and the Isle of Orleans to France, and France in turn ceding to Spain parts of Tuscany (an area that would then be granted to the King of Spain's son-in-law).[14]

The United States was unaware Spain had returned Louisiana to France. When French officials closed the Port of New Orleans to American citizens and forbade trade, President Thomas Jefferson sent his Minister to France, Robert Livingston, and future United States President James Monroe to negotiate a deal. The result of the negotiations was the LOUISIANA PURCHASE OF 1803 in which the United States paid just over twelve million dollars for 828,000 square miles of land known as the Louisiana Territory. The Louisiana Purchase infuriated Spain, which in turn filed a protest against France for selling Louisiana to the United States. But a "deal was a deal" and even though Spain had originally ceded the Isle of Orleans and present-day Louisiana to France, the country had no authority to undo the purchase agreement between the United States and France.[15]

The Louisiana Purchase did not specify the exact boundaries of the land the United States gained in the purchase. (The Lewis and Clark expedition did not begin until the following year.) Old French maps had, however, charted the area from West Florida along the Gulf Coast into present day Alabama, Mississippi, and Louisiana, and the United States claimed the entire area.[16] Spain disputed the United States' claim of ownership of the area since the Louisiana Purchase did not define the exact parameters of the land the United States had purchased, and many individuals saw the area—particularly that of present-day east and central Texas—as essentially "up for grabs." Among the individuals ready to take up arms and lay claim to the land were the Mexican revolutionary Bernardo Gutierrez and U. S. Army officer Augustus Magee. In 1812, the GUTIERREZ-MAGEE EXPEDITION led a filibustering campaign to liberate Texas from Spanish rule. The expedition first assembled near Natchitoches, Louisiana. Armed with a militia of about 130 men, the expedition crossed the Sabine River, entered Nacogdoches, and continued to travel into present-day central Texas. After successfully seizing Presido La Bahia (near present-day Goliad), the expedition grew to a force of about 800 men and surged west into San Antonio. On March 29, 1813, the revolutionaries defeated a Spanish royalist army in the Battle of Rosillo. The battle was followed by a rapid series of bungled plots, allegiances, and alliances, and the Spanish army firmly defeated the revolutionaries five months later in the BATTLE OF MEDINA. Among those fighting for Spain in both the Battle of Rosillo and the Battle of Medina was a young Spanish lieutenant named ANTONIO LOPEZ DE SANTA ANNA. Santa Anna was cited for bravery at the Battle of Medina and quickly rose through the ranks of the Spanish army.

The Gutierrez-Magee Expedition lasted only about a year, but it reinforced the idea that complete peace in Texas could not be restored.[17] Unrest and invasion continued for the next six years despite the fact that the question of "ownership" of Texas was settled by the ADAMS-ONIS TREATY OF 1819. The Adams-Onis Treaty clearly established the Sabine River as the boundary between the United States and Spain and granted all of Florida to the United States and all of Texas to Spain. The treaty did not quell the desires of some individuals to "liberate" Texas. On June 8, 1819, a group of 120 Anglo fighters led by Eli Harris crossed the Sabine River and traveled on to Nacogdoches to meet up with James Long, a Natchez, Mississippi, merchant and doctor. The troops established a provisional government, or "Supreme Council," in Nacogdoches, and declared Long its chief. The Council then proclaimed Galveston a port of entry, authorized the construction of a fort at Point Bolivar, and declared Jean Lafitte governor of the Bolivar Peninsula and Galveston Island. By July, Long had enlisted more than 300 men under his command and appealed to Laffite for assistance. When both Lafitte and the Supreme Council in Nacogdoches failed to deliver aid, Long fled to Point Bolivar where he established his headquarters and attempted to reorganize his forces. Spain quickly called out troops to put down the LONG EXPEDITION, and Long and fifty-two men left Point Bolivar and traveled inland in hopes of capturing La Bahia. At La Bahia, Spanish forces soundly defeated the expedition and Long was taken prisoner, sent to Mexico City, and later shot and killed by a prison guard.[18]

The Wild and Wonderful Women of Texas: Jane Wilkinson Long (1798–1880) and "Kian" (birth unknown; death unknown)

JANE LONG, the wife of James Long (the Long Expedition), traveled from Natchez, Mississippi, to Nacogdoches with her two children and KIAN, a slave girl (whose birth name, birthdate, and family are unknown). The group then traveled from Nacogdoches to Point Bolivar to join Jane's husband at his military fort. They arrived at Point Bolivar in 1821. Soon after their arrival on Bolivar, Long left his pregnant wife, their surviving daughter (one child died along the way), and 12-year-old Kian on the peninsula to continue his military activities.

The three females remained at Point Bolivar—alone—after all others had left and together survived a severe winter with little food or protection. Jane gave birth in the deep cold of December with only young Kian to assist in the delivery. Somehow, Kian was able to find enough food to keep the women alive.[19] In 1822, Jane received word that her husband had died, and when the child she had delivered with Kian's help also died, Jane, her surviving daughter (Ann), and Kian left Point Bolivar and traveled to San Antonio, then back to Natchez, then back to Texas.

In 1827, Jane became a member of Austin's Colony and received land in present-day Waller County.[20] Together the women opened a boarding house near present-day Brazoria, and Jane subsequently secured another tract of land near present-day Richmond. There, Jane and Kian (Ann had since married) developed a plantation, raised cattle, and grew cotton.[21] Jane Long thereby became one of Texas' first Anglo women business entrepreneurs.

It is reported that Jane Long was courted by Texas patriots Sam Houston, Mirabeau B. Lamar, and Ben Milam. Her life might have been made "more comfortable" by marriage given the harsh Texas climate of the 1830s; however, she refused to "settle" and some historical accounts claim Long broke Milam's heart because she refused to remarry.[22] Kian remained with Jane after emancipation and upon her death (date unknown), Kian's granddaughter, also named Kian, came to live with Jane. Jane died in 1880.[23] Kian's descendants were reported in the 1900 U.S. Census to be living in the Richmond area[24] but no subsequent accounts are recorded.

Austin's Colony (1821–1836)

The Long Expedition and the Gutierrez-Magee Expedition failed to secure Texas independence from Spain. But, some Anglo-Americans continued to hold an interest in Texas regardless of whether the United States or Spain controlled the area. The first person to obtain official permission to bring Anglo-American settlers into Spanish Texas was MOSES AUSTIN. A Connecticut-born, Philadelphia dry-goods business owner, Austin extended his business to Richmond, Virginia, and in 1789 secured a contract to roof the Virginia state capitol in lead. When both his Philadelphia and Virginia businesses began to fail, Austin looked toward the rumored lead deposits in Spanish Upper Louisiana and began developing a plan to settle an Anglo-American colony in Spanish Texas. Austin traveled to San Antonio, and upon his arrival in 1820 was treated to a dinner meeting hosted by the Spanish governor. As fate would have it, Austin recognized at the meeting the BARON DE BASTROP, whom Austin had met almost twenty years earlier in New Orleans. Bastrop, a native of Louisiana,[25] had since settled in San Antonio and gained significant prestige among the city's residents and Spanish officials. When Bastrop heard the enthusiasm with which Austin spoke of his colonization plan, he worked on Austin's behalf to secure permission for him to establish the colony. On December 26, 1820, Spanish Governor Martínez endorsed and forwarded Moses Austin's colonization plan to higher authorities in Spain.[26]

For the Record: Baron de Bastrop (1759–1827)

Barron de Bastrop was born Philip Hendrik Nering Bögel in Paramaribo, Dutch Guiana, on November 23, 1759. He moved to Holland with his parents in 1764, and in 1779 enlisted in the cavalry of Holland and Upper Issel. He was later appointed tax collector of the region. In 1793, Bogel was accused of embezzling tax funds, fled Holland, and adopted the title "Baron de Bastrop." Bastrop arrived in Spanish Louisiana in 1795 and fully presented himself as a Dutch nobleman.[27]

After Louisiana was sold to the United States in 1803, Bastrop moved to Spanish Texas and settled in San Antonio. There, he flaunted his faux nobility, established a freighting business, and gained influence among the city's officials and residents. The settlers of Austin's Colony elected Bastrop to the provincial government at San Antonio in 1823, which in turn chose him as representative to the legislature of the new state of Coahuila y Tejas. While serving in the capitol at Saltillo, Mexico, Bastrop was instrumental in the passage of an act establishing a port at Galveston.

Bastrop died on February 23, 1827, and was buried in Saltillo. Historian Richard W. Moore writes that although Bastrop's "pretensions to nobility were not universally accepted at face value even in his own lifetime, he earned respect as a diplomat and legislator." The city and county of Bastrop, Texas, and city of Bastrop, Louisiana, were named in his honor.[28]

Austin returned home to Virginia to await word. Unfortunately, he contracted pneumonia, either while in Texas or during his journey home, and received news on his deathbed that permission for his colony had been granted. His dying wish was that his wife make sure their son, Stephen Fuller Austin, fulfilled his colonization plan.[29] STEPHEN F. AUSTIN set out for San Antonio de Bexar shortly after his father's death on June 10, 1821, and upon his arrival was declared the rightful heir to his father's grant. The grant allowed Austin to settle 300 families—later known as the OLD THREE HUNDRED—in Spanish Texas. Austin selected the rich river bottom between the Brazos and Colorado Rivers, south of the *El Camino Real*, as the land upon which to establish Austin's Colony. The settlement of AUSTIN'S COLONY from 1821 to 1836 has been called the most successful colonization movement in American history. The grant opened up a flood of American immigrants, and by 1835 as many as 30,000 had arrived at Austin's Colony.[30] The settlement also brought Anglo and African settlers from the United States into contact with "the governmental and ranching traditions of Spain and Mexico [and] helped set the course for much of Texas' history in the 19th century."[31]

Conclusion

Early Texas history is filled with intriguing individuals and events that helped shape the state's future. The settlement of Austin's Colony marked the beginning of significant Anglo immigration into the state. But, Native American Indians had roamed the lands of present-day Texas for hundreds of centuries before the arrival of Europeans in the early 1500s, and Spain had ruled Texas for three centuries before Anglo settlement began in earnest. Chapter 2 explores immigration into Texas by a number of Anglo groups as well as African movements into Texas beginning with the settlement of Austin's Colony.

Key Terms

Alonso Alvarez de Pineda
Angelina
First official Spanish Settlements
Louisiana Purchase of 1803
Battle of Medina
Adams-Onis Treaty of 1819
Jane Long
Moses Austin
Stephen F. Austin
Austin's Colony

Esteban
Jean Lafitte
Treaty of Fontainebleau
Gutierrez-Magee Expedition
Antonio Lopez de Santa Anna
Long Expedition
Kian
Baron de Bastrop
Old Three Hundred

Chapter 2

Migration and Immigration to Texas

Chapter 2 examines early migration and immigration into Texas. Upon completing the chapter, you should be able to demonstrate knowledge about:

- ▸ Patterns of immigration into Austin's Colony
- ▸ Early African and African-American movements into Texas
- ▸ Texas settlement patterns by specific immigrant groups
- ▸ Early settlements and communities in Texas
- ▸ The names of key individuals and the settlement of Texas

Austin's Colony

The vast majority of Anglo-Americans that arrived at Austin's Colony were of British ancestry,[32] but a number of Irish colonists were also counted among the original settlers.[33] Most of the Old Three Hundred were farmers by trade and tended to arrive in Texas as independent, single family units instead of in groups.[34] The largest numbers had migrated from the Trans-Appalachian South and were part of a larger trend in early 19th century America toward westward migration.[35] Stephen F. Austin, in an effort to avoid controversy and conflict among the colonists, generally accepted into his colony only those who were of "higher" economic standing, and several families including the Bells (British), Bordens (British), Kuykendalls (Dutch), and Rabbs (Austrian) already possessed substantial economic means before they arrived at Austin's Colony. Furthermore, only four of the original 300 grantees were illiterate[36] and a large number were slaveholders when they arrived and brought their slaves to the colony. By the fall of 1825, sixty-nine of the families in Austin's Colony owned a total of 443 slaves, which accounted for nearly a quarter of the colony's total population of 1,790.[37]

African and African-American Movements into Texas

The arrival of slaves at Austin's Colony increased the number of Africans living in Texas but did not mark the beginning of African movement into Texas. Beginning with Esteban's arrival in 1528 as the slave of a member of de Vaca's crew, African movements into Texas increased largely as a result of slaveholders bringing indentured servants into the area. Under Spanish rule, free blacks were accepted socially and permitted to work in professions or skilled trades, and under Mexican rule they had all the legal and political rights of citizenship.[38] Even though the Mexican government legally abolished slavery in 1829, there were approximately 5,000 enslaved people living in Texas in early 1830,[39] and by the time Texas became a republic in 1836, slavery was an established and thriving institution that subjugated approximately 13,000 African people.[40]

The Constitution of the Republic of Texas (the CONSTITUTION OF 1836), gave preference to Anglo-American settlers, protected the rights of Anglo people in the unoccupied lands of the republic, and, more significantly, made specific exemptions of Africans and the descendants of Africans and Indians from state citizenship. In early February 1840, the Republic of Texas passed *An Act Concerning Free Persons of Color*. The act held that unless the Congress of the Republic ruled that a petitioner could stay, all free non-white persons were required to leave the state by January 1, 1842, or be sold into slavery. Furthermore, any free non-white person caught entering Texas would be arrested, jailed, and put up for public auction if a $1,000 bail wasn't paid.[41] The act, combined with the Republic's constitutional protection of the ownership of both slaves and land, created an incentive for southerners in the Deep South to expand the system of slavery westward into Texas. The number of slaves in Texas rose dramatically from 5,000 in 1830 to over 182,000 by the end of the Civil War.[42]

Emancipation for African-American people living in Texas was announced on June 19, 1865. In an effort to place severe restrictions on the rights of newly emancipated black Texans, the Texas legislature passed a series of laws that included "Black Codes," Jim Crow laws, poll taxes, literacy tests, and restrictive covenants. In 1867, the United States Congress eliminated the Black Codes and ushered in a new phase of Reconstruction in Texas. African Americans made substantial contributions to the transition of Texas from a slave-labor state. Ten African-American delegates at the Constitutional Convention of 1868–1869 helped to write a new state constitution that protected civil rights, established the state's first public education system, and extended the franchise to all men regardless of race. Forty-one African-American Texans served in the Texas legislature between 1868 and 1900.[43] After the Civil War, many African-American Texans moved from the state's rural areas to cities such as Dallas, Austin, Houston, and San Antonio. The townships they established on the outskirts of urban cities were referred to as "freedmen towns," which became distinct African-American communities.[44] Some of the freedmen town communities still exist today including "Deep Ellum" in Dallas,[45] and the Fourth Ward, later known as "Little Harlem," in Houston.[46]

For the Record: The Texas Origins of "Juneteenth"

On June 19, 1865, Union Major General Gordon Granger arrived in Galveston and issued GENERAL ORDER NO. 3, which read in part: "The people of Texas are informed that, in accordance with a proclamation from the Executive of the United States, all slaves are free."[47]

News of emancipation traveled slowly to Texas, and by the time General Order No. 3 was announced, the "Executive" to whom Granger was referring, President Abraham Lincoln, was dead. The 13th Amendment abolishing slavery was well on its way to ratification and the Emancipation Proclamation ending slavery in the Confederacy (at least on paper) had taken effect two-and-a-half years prior to the announcement of the Order in Texas.[48]

Despite its long delayed arrival, General Order No. 3 by no means signaled the instant freedom of most of the Lone Star State's 250,000 slaves. Plantation masters decided when and how to announce freedom to their slaves and it was not uncommon for them to delay the news until after the harvest. In Galveston, the ex-Confederate mayor flouted the Army by forcing freed people back to work,[49] and terror and violence toward blacks followed the announcement of the order. Freed black men and women in Texas nonetheless transformed June 19th from a date marking the announcement of an unheeded military order into a day of celebration described as "one of the most inspiring grassroots efforts of the post-Civil War period."[50]

The first "JUNETEENTH" celebration was held in 1866—exactly one year after the announcement of Order No. 3 in Texas[51]—and a larger celebration was held in Austin the following year.[52] Ex-slaves in many parts of Texas purchased land, or "emancipation grounds," specifically for the purpose of holding Juneteenth gatherings. Some of the originally purchased property still serves as gathering places for Juneteenth celebrations including Emancipation Park in Houston (purchased in 1872), Comanche Crossing—now known as Booker T. Washington Park—in Mexia (purchased in 1898), and Emancipation Park in East Austin (purchased in 1907).

The celebration of Juneteenth spread from Texas to the neighboring states of Louisiana, Arkansas, and Oklahoma, and then to Alabama, Florida, and California as African-American Texans migrated after emancipation.[53] Today, Juneteenth celebrations are held in most if not all of the 50 states, and almost all states now have some form of legislation or declaration establishing Juneteenth as a state holiday or day of recognition.[54]

Spanish and Spanish Canary Islander Immigration to Texas

The Spanish Colonial era in Texas began around 1689 with the systematic establishment of missions and presidios (the secular counterparts to missions), designed to spread Christianity and establish Spanish control over the region.[55] The first Spanish missions were established in the 1680s near present-day San Angelo, El Paso, and Presidio—areas that were closely tied to settlements in what is today New Mexico. In 1690, Spanish missions spread into East Texas after news surfaced of La Salle's incursion into the area. In East Texas, the Spanish settlers encountered the Caddo Indians, whom they called "Tejas" (derived from the Caddoan word "Tay-yas," meaning friend).[56] Evidence of the early Spanish mission and presidio system can still be seen today with the Alamo in San Antonio; the remains of Mission San Antonio Valero and nearby La Villita in and near San Antonio; La Bahía, which includes a presidio and missions, near present-day Goliad; and Los Adaes (which served as the capital of Spanish Texas) near present-day Robeline, Louisiana.[57]

Founded in 1718 as a combination of civilian, military, and mission communities, SAN ANTONIO DE BÉXAR (originally settled as San Fernando de Béxar) proved to be the most successful Spanish presidio system in Texas. The earliest settlers to San Antonio were Spanish Canary Islanders. A year after San Antonio was founded, the Marqués de San Miguel de Aguayo made a report to the king of Spain proposing that families be transported from the Canary Islands, Galicia, and Havana to populate the province of Texas. His plan was approved, and under the leadership of Juan Leal Goraz, a group of fifty-six Canary Islanders (fifteen families) traveled by ship and then proceeded overland to San Antonio de Béxar, where they arrived on March 9, 1731.[58] The Canary Island immigrants formed the nucleus of the villa of SAN FERNANDO DE BÉXAR, the first regularly organized civil government in Texas.[59]

Spanish royal authorities continued their efforts to increase immigration into Texas in hopes that civilian settlements consisting of artisans, farmers, and traders would help offset the growing expense of maintaining Spanish military installations and presidios throughout Texas.[60] From 1773 until 1824 when Texas was joined to the Mexican state of Coahuila, royal authorities lured an additional 400 families of Canary Islanders to Texas by offering them generous land grants and the right to carry the official title of *hidalgo*, or noble.[61] Today, several old families of San Antonio can trace their descent from the Canary Island colonists.[62] And, the claim can easily be made that without the influence of Canary Islanders, the state's famous "Tex-Mex" cuisine would be far less flavorful. The immigrants brought with them the spices of their homeland—cilantro, cumin, and chile peppers—and combined them with local ingredients like beef, onions, pecans, pinto beans, and the flavor of mesquite wood to produce a distinct brand of Texas cooking.[63]

The Wild and Wonderful Women of Texas: María Gertrudis Pérez (1790–1832)

MARIA GERTRUDIS PEREZ (also known as Maria Perez Cassiano), was a descendent of the Canary Islanders that in the 18th century formed the first organized civil government in Texas. She was born in 1790 in the family homestead at the Royal Presidio of San Antonio de Béxar, and at the age of 24, married a man almost forty years her senior. Her husband, an experienced military commander and Governor of the State of Coahuila, was often gone on military expeditions in the western Mexican provinces.[64]

Important to the story of both Maria Perez and the history of Texas women is the fact that Spanish law in 1814—and later the Constitution of Coahuila y Tejas of 1827—allowed women community and individual property rights, which meant that women were considered by law to be equal to men in terms of inheritance, property ownership, and property administration.

During her wealthy and influential husband's frequent absences, Maria would fully assume his duties and administer his estate. Known as "La Brigaviella" (the Brigadier General), Maria regularly dressed in an embroidered military jacket and reviewed on horseback the troops in San Antonio's Military Plaza.[65]

Native American Indians in Texas

Native American Indian tribes roamed Texas for many centuries prior to the arrival of Europeans. All areas of the state contain rich histories about Native American Indian tribes indigenous to their region, but one area plays a particularly significant role in understanding the plight of Native Americans after European invasion. Located in the north central section of the Texas Panhandle, present-day Hutchinson County is now extremely arid due to a drastic decline in the water table; however, the region was once filled with many springs fed by the Canadian River that sustained abundant wildlife—including herds of thousands of buffalo.[66] Hutchinson County is the site of ADOBE WALLS, the name given to a couple of trading posts built by Anglo settlers around 1843. Indian raids along the Santa Fe Trail prompted the commanding general of the Department of New Mexico to send a military team led by Colonel Christopher "Kit" Carson to "punish" the Kiowa and Comanche tribes for the raids. Carson and his men attacked a Kiowa village in November 1864, and then retired to Adobe Walls to rest. There, more than 1,000 members of the Kiowa and Comanche tribes launched an unsuccessful counter-attack against Carson's well-armed militia.[67] The Indians' defeat at the First Battle of Adobe Walls signaled an "all clear" for Anglo merchants and buffalo hunters to pour into the area. Merchants from Dodge City, Kansas, followed buffalo hunters into the Texas Panhandle and established a large complex at Adobe Walls that included a corral, restaurant, stores, and saloons to serve the 200–300 buffalo hunters that roamed the area.[68]

Early in the morning of June 27, 1874, a combined force of some 700 Comanche, Cheyenne, Kiowa, and Arapaho warriors led by Comanche CHIEF QUANAH PARKER attacked the buffalo camp. The camp was inhabited by only 28 Anglo men—including William Barclay "Bat" Masterson and William "Billy" Dixon—at the time of the attack, but the Indian warriors were virtually defenseless against the hunters' superior weapons. An estimated 70 Indians were killed and Chief Parker was wounded.[69] The Second Battle of Adobe Walls was a crushing defeat for the Indian tribes, but they nonetheless continued to raid in desperate and final attempts to retain their ancestral and spiritual homelands. The RED RIVER WAR (1874–75) marked the final chapter in the centuries-long history of Native American sovereignty in Texas. On June 2, 1875, the Comanche Indians and Chief Parker surrendered at Fort Sill (near present-day Lawton, Oklahoma).[70] The surrender is significant to Texas history for a number of reasons: it was the final subjugation by Anglos of the powerful Comanche, Kiowa, and southern Cheyenne Indians; it marked the virtual extinction of the southern herd of buffalo; and, it signaled the opening of the Texas Panhandle to white settlement and the accompanying West Texas ranching industry.[71] The Red River War also resulted in the final relocation of the Southern Plains Indians onto reservations as the United States government forced the last Indians living east of the Pecos River into the Oklahoma territory.

For the Record: Chief Quanah Parker (ca. 1845–1911)

The exact birthplace of Chief Quanah Parker is disputed. Some historians claim he was born on Elk Creek south of the Wichita Mountains in what is now Oklahoma, and others claim his birthplace was near Cedar Lake southeast of Seminole, Texas.[72] He was the son of Peta Nocona, a noted war chief of the Noconi band of Comanche, and Cynthia Ann Parker, an Anglo woman captured in 1836 during a Comanche raid on Parker's Fort (near present-day Groesbeck, Texas). Cynthia Parker converted to the Indian way of life and remained with the Noconi Comanche for 24 years.

In 1860, the Texas Rangers and a militia led by Ranger Captain "Sul" Ross raided a Comanche encampment on the Pease River (near present-day Quanah, Texas, in Foard County) in retaliation against recent Comanche attacks on white settlers. Chief Peta Nocona was killed in the raid and Quanah Parker's mother and sister were captured and incarcerated. The battle decimated the Noconi band and forced Quanah, now an orphan, to take refuge with the Quahada Comanches of the Llano Estacado.[73]

Parker and the Quahadas were able to hold the Texas plains against the United States Cavalry for several years in the 1850s and 1860s. But, as the Indians' primary source of subsistence—buffalo—was being decimated by Anglo hunters pouring into the region, Parker and the Quahadas formed a multi-tribal alliance dedicated to expelling the hunters from the plains. The two battles of Adobe Walls proved disastrous to the alliance and within a year the Quahadas surrendered their independence at the Red River War and moved to the Kiowa-Comanche reservation in southwestern Oklahoma.[74]

In an attempt to unite the various Comanche bands in Oklahoma, federal agents named Quanah Parker chief, and the Kiowa-Comanche acquiesced to the government's bestowment of the honor. Over the next quarter century, Chief Parker worked to promote self-sufficiency and self-reliance by supporting the construction of schools on reservation lands and promoting the creation of a ranching industry by entering into agreements with Anglo ranchers to allow them to lease grazing lands within the Comanche reservation. However, a growing movement to strip the Comanche of their lands resulted in the federal government's dissolution of the Kiowa-Comanche reservation in 1901. For the remaining years of his life, Parker owned and operated a profitable ranch and became very wealthy as the result of shrewd investments.[75]

Chief Parker adopted some of the Anglo ways of life, but he never cut his braids and remained a member of the Native American Church credited with introducing and encouraging the use of peyote among the tribes in Oklahoma (despite the fact that his son, White Parker, became a Methodist minister). He died on February 23, 1911, and was buried beside his mother in the Post Oak Mission Cemetery near Cache, Oklahoma. In 1957, the expansion of a missile base forced the relocation of the Post Oak Mission Cemetery and the reburial of Quanah and Cynthia Ann Parker in the Fort Sill Post Cemetery at Lawton, Oklahoma. On August 9, 1957, Quanah was buried with full military honors in a section of that cemetery now known as Chief's Knoll.[76]

Forced migration of Native American Indians into Oklahoma had occurred before the Red River War largely as a result of Indian defeats during armed conflicts such as the Battle of the Neches in Van Zandt and Henderson counties, near present-day Chandler.[77] After Texas entered the Union in 1845, the federal government assumed control of Indian affairs but had no authority to create reservations in Texas since the state retained ownership of all public lands. In 1852, the Texas legislature passed a bill authorizing the governor to work with the federal government to set aside Texas land reserved for Indian resettlement. A few Texas reservation attempts failed to work because Native Americans had neither the desire nor the intention to relocate to the assigned areas. Three resettlement attempts did, however, prove successful. The ALABAMA-COUSHATTA INDIANS, described as having "some sort of genius for peace and diplomacy,"[78] remained distant from conflicts during the long period of Native American-Anglo animosity in Texas. Even Mirabeau B. Lamar, a consummate foe of Native Americans, publically stated that the Alabama-Coushatta tribes should be guaranteed occupancy of land in Texas.[79] In 1854, the state legislature appropriated money for the purchase of 1,280 acres of land in Polk County to be reserved for Alabama Indians and Coushatta Indians, in a combined reservation.[80] In addition to the Alabama-Coushatta Reservation, two Native American Indian reservations continue to exist in Texas—one occupied by the Tigua Indians in the city limits of El Paso and Ysleta in El Paso County, and another by the Kickapoo Indians on the Rio Grande close to present-day Eagle Pass.[81] The oldest of the three reservations, the Alabama-Coushatta, is the only one to have had land guarantees by the Republic of Texas republic, the State of Texas, and the United States government.

German Immigration and Settlement

The non-Spanish European ethnic group to make the greatest impact on Texas was German. The German-Texan culture started in 1831 when FREDERICK ERNST, "Father of German Immigration to Texas," received a grant of more than 4,000 acres in present-day Austin County.[82] In 1840, the *ADELSVEREIN*—the Society for the Protection of German Immigrants in Texas—was created in Germany, and through the Society's sponsorship, thousands of Germans immigrated to Texas. Upon their arrival in Galveston or Indianola,[83] the immigrants traveled to Houston and then on to the valleys between the Brazos and Colorado rivers. Most of the original German immigrants to Texas settled in Central Texas around present-day New Braunfels and Fredericksburg.[84] German immigration and migration exploded after Texas entered the Union in 1845, and until 1877 German speakers in the city of San Antonio outnumbered both Hispanics and Anglos.[85]

For the Record: Indianola, Texas

INDIANOLA, originally named "Indian Point," was founded on Matagorda Bay in present-day Calhoun County in August 1846 by the commissioner general of the *Adelsverein*, as the landing place for German immigrants bound for western Texas under the sponsorship of the Society.

Indianola played a crucial role in the early history of Texas. It served as the chief port through which European and American immigrants flowed into western Texas; was an essential deep-water port during the Mexican War; served as an army supply depot to frontier forts in western Texas; was the terminus for Charles Morgan's New York-based steamship line; was the beginning point of a military road that led to San Antonio, Austin, and Chihuahua; and was the landing place of the "camel experiment" (1855–1863) designed to transport military supplies into the American southwest.

Indianola was second only to Galveston as the largest port in Texas, until a catastrophic hurricane hit the port in 1875. The town was again hit by a hurricane in 1886, and by 1887 the site had been abandoned. Indianola is now a ghost town marked only by a historical marker commissioned by the Texas Historical Commission.[86]

Many German-Texans were staunch opponents of slavery. Under the leadership of FREIER MANN VEREIN, the Freeman's Association was established in Texas and the issue of German opposition gained public attention during the annual *Staats-Saengerfest* (State Singers Festival) held in San Antonio in May 1854.[87] The association adopted a platform that declared slavery an evil and asserted that the United States government should help the states to abolish slavery.[88] During the time the Freeman's Association was established in the state, German-Texas freemasons, freethinkers, political activists, and liberals migrated to the banks of Cypress Creek in Kendall County, where in 1854 the town of Comfort, known for its Union sentiment during the Civil War, was established.[89]

Czech and Slovak Immigration

Down the road from Comfort was New Ulm, a community consisting largely of Czech and Slovak immigrants. Czech immigration to Texas did not begin in earnest until the 1850s, with the first group arriving in Galveston in 1852. Most Czech immigrants had been farmers and poor laborers in Europe, so they settled in areas that contained land rich for farming. Most of the early Czech immigrants to Texas settled near present-day La Grange in the area around Fayetteville, often referred to as the "cradle of Czech immigration,"[90] and along the coastal plains near present-day Wharton, Victoria, and Fort Bend.[91] Others traveled west to present-day Shiner, north to present-day Snook, and on into the "blackland prairie" that runs from Williamson through Bell and McClennan counties with settlements concentrating in present-day Temple and West.[92] The Texas Czechs became known for their methods of cultivation and played a major role in the Texas cotton industry.[93]

Irish and Scotch Irish Immigration

Immigration from Ireland to Texas was already underway when Stephen F. Austin received his father's grant to establish the Old Three Hundred colony. Dublin-born Hugh O'Connor arrived in Texas sometime in the early 1760s and upon arrival changed his name to the more Spanish "HUGO OCONOR." Selected to serve as the Spanish governor of Texas from 1767 to 1770,[94] Oconor paved the way for other Irish immigrants to settle in Texas. A number of Irish-born Spanish subjects were counted in the Nacogdoches census in the late 1700s, and Irish immigration increased in 1828 when two separate pairs of Irish empresarios founded colonies in Texas. John McMullen and James McGloin established the San Patricio Colony south of San Antonio; and James Power and James Hewetson established the Refugio Colony on the Gulf Coast. The two colonies were settled mainly by Irish immigrants, but Mexicans and immigrants of other nationalities were also welcomed into the settlements.[95] Following the lead set by Oconor, Irish settlers immigrated to San Antonio in such large numbers that by the mid-1800s the area around the Alamo was dubbed (and is still referred to as) "Irish Flats."[96]

Texas history is filled with an impressive list of Texans descending from Irish, Scottish, or Scotch-Irish ancestry including Sam Houston, Stephen F. Austin, Davy Crockett, and Jim Bowie.[97] Scottish immigration particularly increased in the late 1800s after ranching came to define the state's economy with "eager and ambitious Scots [coming] directly from Edinburgh and Aberdeen to raise cattle and build railroads—and make money."[98]

French Immigration

In addition to English, Irish, and Scottish immigration, French settlers immigrated into Spanish Texas. Beginning with La Salle's arrival near Sabine Pass and the establishment of Fort Saint Louis,[99] French settlers including Creoles, Cajuns, refugees from slave uprisings in Santo Domingo, and emigres from the French Revolution came to Texas after the signing of the Louisiana Purchase.[100] The "pirate republic" established on Galveston Island by Frenchman Jean Lafitte contained more than 1,000 persons at its peak in 1818,[101] but Lafitte held no interest in assisting his French brethren with immigration and settlement and remained focused on his privateering business. The father of French immigration to Texas was HENRI CASTRO, who in 1844 founded a French settlement now known as Castroville. Born in Landes, France, Castro's family descended from Portuguese Jews who had fled to France after the inception of the Spanish Inquisition. Castro immigrated to the United States, and in 1842 entered into a contract with the Republic of Texas government to settle a colony in Southwest Texas on the Medina River. From 1843 to 1847, Castro brought to Texas almost 2,000 French immigrants[102] consisting of 485 families and 457 single men.[103] A wise, learned, and humane man, Castro used his own money to improve the welfare of his colonists, furnishing them with cows, farm implements, seeds, and medicine.[104] Out of gratitude for his influence and kindness to Texas, the first President of the Republic of Texas, Sam Houston, appointed Castro consul general for Texas in Paris, France. Castro County, in the Texas Panhandle, was named in his honor.[105]

For the Record: *Los Adaes*, Don Antonio Gil Y'Barbo, and Nacogdoches: A Story of Spanish, French, and Native American Life in Deep East Texas

LOS ADAES, located near present-day Robeline, Louisiana, included both a mission (founded in 1717) and a presidio (established in 1721). It was the easternmost establishment in Spanish Texas for more than half a century.

The original purpose of Los Adaes was to block the French from encroaching into Spain's southwestern lands. The major trail west, the El Camino Real, was barely a footpath at the time, and the mission's remote location in east Texas (now Louisiana) was isolated and far removed from the centers of Spanish government emerging in San Antonio de Bexar and La Bahia (Goliad). Out of necessity, the inhabitants of Los Adaes turned to the French at nearby Natchitoches, Louisiana, on the Red River, for food supplies. Despite trade prohibitions by Spanish authorities, the Spanish *Adaesenos*, the Louisiana French, and the friendly local Caddo-speaking Indians, the Adaes (for whom the mission was named), developed a system of commerce, trade, and friendship.[106]

When possession of French Louisiana was transferred to Spain in 1762 (the Treaty of Fontainebleau), the Spanish crown ordered the inhabitants of Los Adaes (estimated at 500) to abandon the site and move to San Antonio.[107] Those who survived the long and treacherous trip to San Antonio found the city did not suit their frontier sensibilities, and they sought permission to leave the city and return to East Texas.

During the Adaesenos' stay in San Antonio, DON ANTONIO GIL Y'BARBO emerged as the group's most influential member and soon caught the attention of Spanish Governor Domingo Cabello. Y'Barbo, born and raised at Presidio Los Adaes, had followed in his father's footsteps and served as a member of the Spanish military at the presidio.[108] During his many years at Los Adaes, Y'Barbo had forged close commercial and social relationships with both the local Caddo Indians and the French at the Natchitoches.[109] The Governor named Y'Barbo principal trader and Indian agent to the Louisiana-Texas borderlands,[110] and the Adaesenos left San Antonio. Stopping along the Old San Antonio Road (in current Madison County), an epidemic and subsequent Comanche raid ravaged their new settlement, and the surviving Adaesenos again began moving north and east.[111]

Y'Barbo and the Adaesenos eventually settled in Nacogdoches in Spring 1779. First established as a Spanish settlement in 1716, NACOGDOCHES (named for the Nacogdoche Indians, a Caddo Indian group) had become a gateway for trade—mostly illicit—with the French.[112] Y'Barbo was appointed Lieutenant-Governor of the settlement of Nacogdoches in October 1779, and with his appointment to the post the Spanish government effectively "legalized" Nacogdoches as a permanent town in Spanish Texas.

Y'Barbo became a "powerful commercial, diplomatic, and cultural broker indispensable to the survival of Spanish colonization in East Texas amidst perpetual warfare to the west."[113] The strong ties Y'Barbo and the Adaesenos had with the French and the Caddos on the Louisiana-Texas borderlands "played an instrumental role in the reversal of Spanish policy toward the Lipan Apaches and laid the foundation upon which peace negotiations with the Comanches became possible."[114] Y'Barbo laid out Nacogdoches streets with the intersection of El Camino Real and El Calle del Norte serving as the town's center; established a ranch, La Lucana, on the Attoyac River in Nacogdoches County; and built a stone trading house that is today called the "Old Stone Fort." The trading house became a "gateway from the United States to the vast Texas Frontier."[115] Y'Barbo died at his ranch in 1809.[116]

Conclusion

Migration, immigration, and movements into Texas had a profound impact on the political culture that shaped the Texas Constitution of 1876 (the state's current constitution). Knowledge of early migration and immigration patterns sets the stage for understanding the connections Texans hold to the land and the resources it contains as well as later migrations into Texas in the 20th and 21st centuries. Chapter 3 examines the constitutions Texas has had throughout its history and the political cultures that produced each constitution. Current state demographics are also discussed, especially in terms of how the state's economy has influenced recent migration.

Key Terms

Demographics of Austin's Colony
Constitution of 1836
Juneteenth
San Antonio de Béxar

African Movements into Texas
General Order No. 3
Spanish Immigration
San Fernando de Béxar

Maria Gertrudis Perez
Chief Quanah Parker
Alabama-Coushatta Indians
Adelsverein
Freier Mann Verein
Hugo Oconor
Los Adaes
Nacogdoches

Adobe Walls
Red River War
Frederick Ernst
Indianola
Czech and Slovak immigration
Henri Castro
Don Antonio Gil Y'Barbo

Chapter 3

Groundwork for Understanding the Current Texas Constitution (1876): The Constitutions of Texas, Political Culture, and the People of Texas

Chapter 3 completes Unit 1 by outlining the unique features of the various constitutions of Texas (prior to the ratification of the state's current constitution in 1876), the elements of Texas political culture, and current demographic patterns in Texas. Upon completing the chapter, you should be able to demonstrate knowledge about:

- The unique features of each Texas constitution before 1876
- The names of key individuals and the contributions they made to Texas history and politics
- Political culture, especially the elements of Texas political culture
- Demographic patterns in Texas in the 20th and 21st centuries

The Six Flags Flown over Texas

Six flags have flown over Texas, including the Spanish flag, the French flag, the Republic of Texas flag, and the United States flag. Certain cities and settlements in Texas have flown even more flags, including Nacogdoches, which has raised a total of nine flags ranging from the Fredonia Rebellion flag to the Gutierrez-Magee flag and the Long Expedition flag;[117] Laredo, which has flown seven flags, including the short-lived Republic of the Rio Grande flag;[118] and Gonzales, which briefly flew a hastily made flag bearing a white background, a black cannon, and the words "Come and Take It!" over a small, Spanish-made cannon.

For the Record: The "Come and Take It" Flag and the Battle of Gonzales (1835)

The "Come and Take It" flag was an intentional taunt by the Anglo settlers of Gonzales, aimed at the Spanish forces making their way to Gonzales to retrieve a very small cannon. In 1831, the Spanish government had given the settlers the cannon to aid them with defending themselves against Indian attacks.[119]

In 1835, the Spanish military commander of Texas ordered Francisco de Castañeda to travel from San Antonio to Gonzales to retrieve the cannon. Mindful that Texans were already growing tense about the presence of General Antonio Lopez de Santa Anna in Texas, the commander instructed Castañeda to avoid open conflict with the residents of Gonzales, if at all possible.[120] After a very brief skirmish (it really wasn't a "battle" in the truest sense), Castañeda retreated to San Antonio and the cannon remained in the city of Gonzales.

The Battle of Gonzales is considered to be the first battle of the Texas Revolution. In late 1835, the cannon was assigned to a captain in Stephen F. Austin's Texian "Army of the People" and hauled to San Antonio where it remained at the Alamo. No one knows for sure what happened to the cannon, but some historians speculate that General Santa Anna's troops melted it down after the fall of the Alamo.[121]

The first flag to fly over Texas was the Spanish flag. Spain governed Texas for almost three centuries until a series of revolts occurred after Napoleon's invasion and occupation of Spain from 1808 to 1813. Among the revolts was the MEXICAN WAR OF INDEPENDENCE. On September 16, 1810—during the height of Napoleon's occupation of Spain—Father Miguel Hidalgo issued from his pulpit a cry (or *grito*) for the end of Spanish rule in Mexico. In addition to a cry for revolution, Hidalgo's impassioned speech called for the redistribution of land and a concept of racial equality for all people of indigenous descent.[122] Hidalgo then led a militia from the city of Delores, where his church was located, to Mexico City, leaving a bloodbath in his wake. When the militia was defeated at Calderon in 1811, Hidalgo fled north to Chihuahua and was captured and executed by firing squad. Militia members quickly assumed the helm, and rebellion continued throughout the cities and countryside of Mexico. Armies of indigenous and racially mixed revolutionaries fought against the Spanish royalists for the next decade as the *"GRITO DE DELORES"* spurred on the Mexican War of Independence.

Political events unfolding in Spain would greatly influence the outcome of the war. After liberal forces sympathetic to the Mexican revolutionaries gained control of Spain in 1820, formerly staunch royalist Mexican conservatives led by Agustin Iturbide took up the cause of Mexican independence in hopes of retaining their status in Mexico after the country gained independence.[123] Iturbide assumed command of the Mexican army, allied himself with the existing revolutionary forces, and worked with the new representative of the liberal-control Spanish government to devise a plan that would culminate in the TREATY OF CORDOBA, signed on August 21, 1824. The Treaty of Cordoba granted Mexico independence from Spain.

For the Record: The Story of *Cinco de Mayo*

Contrary to the popular belief of many Texans, the Mexican and Mexican-Texan holiday *CINCO DE MAYO* does not mark Mexican independence from Spain (achieved on August 21st, not May 5th). *Cinco de Mayo* marks the day of the anniversary of the BATTLE OF PUEBLA fought during the French-Mexican War.

The year was 1862. The United States was embroiled in the American Civil War, and the country of Mexico was in financial ruin. Mexican President Benito Juarez was forced to default on his country's debts to European governments, and France decided to use the opportunity to expand its empire into Mexico. Late in 1861, a well-armed French fleet (consisting of approximately 6,000 French soldiers) arrived in Veracruz and set out to attack Puebla de Los Angles, a small town in east-central Mexico. President Juarez set up new headquarters in northern Mexico and rounded up a "rag-tag force" of about 2,000 loyal men to go to Puebla to take on the French.[124]

Led by Texas-born General Ignacio Zaragoza (whose birthplace home still stands at the Presidio de La Bahia just outside of Goliad), the Mexican army defeated the French at the Battle of Puebla on May 5,

1862 (*Cinco de Mayo*). The battle itself was not a major strategic victory in the overall war; however, it did symbolize Mexico's ability to defend its sovereignty against the powerful French army under the rule of Napoleon III, and served to tighten Mexican resistance against the French.[125] Six years later, the French army withdrew from Mexico in 1867.[126]

Cinco de Mayo is a huge celebration in Texas because General Zaragoza was born in the state, and in 1999 the Texas Senate declared Goliad the official state annual celebration.[127] The holiday became a nationally celebrated event in the 1960s when Mexican American activists transformed the day into a commemoration of Mexican culture, heritage, and pride in their community.[128] Today, extremely large *Cinco de Mayo* celebrations are held in Los Angeles, Denver, St. Paul, and in Waterfront Park in Portland and Douglas Park in Chicago.[129] The day is, however, a rather minor holiday in Mexico and has never been declared a national holiday. Celebrations are largely confined to the Mexican states of Puebla and Veracruz with *Cinco de Mayo* celebrations that include military reenactments of the Battle of Puebla.[130]

The Treaty of Cordoba contained three primary features: (1) Mexico would be an independent constitutional monarchy; (2) Roman Catholicism would be the official religion of Mexico; and (3) Mexicans of Spanish descent would be given greater rights than Mexicans of mixed or pure Indian blood.[131] Establishing Mexico as an independent constitutional monarchy presented significant challenges primarily due to the fact there were no descendants of the Spanish Bourbon family in Mexico to rule the new nation. Iturbide quickly disposed of the revolutionary forces, placed a crown upon his own head, and became Agustín I, Emperor of Mexico.[132] Iturbide's rule was short lived. Forces led by Antonio Lopez de Santa Anna (whom you will recall had served as a Spanish officer during the defeat of the Magee-Gutierrez Expedition at the Battle of Medina) rose up against Iturbide and, after only ten months on the throne, overthrew the emperor and sent him into exile—first in Italy and then in England. Unaware that the Mexican congress had decreed his death, Iturbide returned to Mexico in 1824 and was executed.[133] Guadalupe Victorio, who fought for Mexican independence alongside Santa Anna, became Mexico's first elected president in 1824 (1824–29). Victorio's presidency focused on foreign relations designed to establish Mexico as an independent country, establishing public finances, and abolishing slavery.[134] Victorio was succeeded by VICENTE GUERRERO, a Mexican revolutionary of African, Mexican, and Indian descent.[135] Guerrero renewed calls for the abolition of slavery; promoted civil rights for all and especially African Mexicans; and called for public schools, land title reforms, and other programs designed to assist the racially and economically oppressed peoples of Mexico.[136] During his presidency, a Spanish expedition attempted to reconquer Mexico and defeated the Mexican army. Guerrero was declared unfit to govern, removed from office, and condemned to death. He was executed in Cuilapan on February 14, 1831.[137]

Constitution of Coahuila y Tejas (1827)—Spanish Texas

The early history of Mexican independence is part of the narrative of Texas history. Certain concepts contained in the Treaty of Cordoba were carried over to Texas' first constitution—the CONSTITUTION OF COAHUILA Y TEJAS, 1827. Under the newly independent Mexican government, the State of Coahuila and the sparsely populated province of Texas were combined. The new state was organized at Saltillo, Mexico, in August 1824, with the Baron de Bastrop representing Texas.[138]

The constitution supported efforts to curtail and limit slavery; created a UNICAMERAL LEGISLATURE charged with promoting education and freedom of the press; and named Roman Catholicism the official religion of Texas. But Texans soon grew discontent with the Mexican federal system and two political conventions were called in San Felipe de Austin in 1832 and 1833. The 1833 convention produced a constitution for a newly proposed state of Texas. When Stephen F. Austin brought the new constitution to the attention of the central government in Mexico City, he was imprisoned by the Mexican government. Austin's imprisonment pushed Texas ever closer to rebellion against Mexico. State political leaders again met in San Felipe in 1835, and a declaration was adopted stating the reasons Texans were beginning to take up arms against Mexico.

In December 1835, a group of Texans overwhelmed the Mexican garrison at THE ALAMO, captured the fort, and seized control of San Antonio. By mid-February 1836, Colonel James Bowie and Lieutenant Colonel William B. Travis had arrived in San Antonio, and Sam Houston was named the newly appointed commander-in-chief of the Texan forces. Houston argued that San Antonio should be abandoned due to an insufficient number of troops, but Bowie and Travis refused to leave. Despite later reinforcements including Davy Crockett, the number of defenders of the Alamo never numbered more than 200.[139] Mexican troops ranging from 1,800 to 6,000 (a large range, but historical estimates vary widely) under the command of General Santa Anna arrived at the Alamo on February 23, 1836, and began a siege of the fort.[140] The Texans held out for 13 days, but Mexican forces breached the outer wall of the courtyard and overpowered the Texans on March 6.

The Mexican army's victory at the Alamo fueled Santa Anna's fervor to conquer Texas. Sam Houston, upon receiving word on March 11 in Gonzales of the fall of the Alamo, retreated to the Colorado River and ordered all inhabitants to accompany him.[141] People all over Texas left everything behind to join Houston's retreat. By March 17, Washington-on-the-Brazos was deserted and by mid-April, Richmond was evacuated as were settlements on both sides of the Brazos River and those located further to the north and east around Nacogdoches and San Augustine.[142] Houston's retreat pressed further toward the Sabine River and, as Texans fled toward Galveston Island and Louisiana, all of the settlements between the Colorado and Brazos Rivers were left unprotected. Known as the RUNAWAY SCRAPE, many former settlers in Texas died as a result of disease, famine, cold, and rain—with most being buried where they fell.[143]

Despite the Runaway Scrape and the Battle of the Alamo (which was still being waged at the time), delegates from each city in Texas met on March 1, 1836, at Washington-on-the-Brazos, and a formal Texas Declaration of Independence for the State of Texas was adopted. The Texas Declaration, much like the national Declaration written by Thomas Jefferson, presented a long list of grievances against the central government in Mexico. The fall of the Alamo on March 6 did not deter the delegates. A second general convention was again held at

Washington-on-the-Brazos in July 1836, and the delegation drafted and passed a new state constitution. By the time the new constitution was written, Sam Houston had gathered some 900 Texan soldiers and again met up with Santa Anna's troops (numbering around 1,250) at the BATTLE OF SAN JACINTO near present-day Houston. Spurred on by cries of "Remember the Alamo!" the Texan forces defeated Santa Anna's army on April 21, 1836. The capture of the commanding general ensured Texas independence. The next day, Santa Anna issued orders for all Mexican troops to pull back behind the Rio Grande River, and on May 14, 1836, Texas officially became an independent republic.[144] As word of the Battle of San Jacinto and Texas independence spread, refugees of the Runaway Scrape began to turn back toward home only to find their homes no longer existed.[145]

The Wild and Wonderful Women of Texas: Emily West (?–?)

EMILY WEST is better known as the "Yellow Rose of Texas." While much of the history of Emily West is shrouded in myth and legend, she is thought to have been an orphan who came to Texas from New York in 1835 with Colonel and Mrs. James Morgan. In Texas, she fell in love with a black man, a musician, thought to be a runaway slave. Bounty hunters and the pressures of the fast-approaching war for independence from Mexico interrupted their relationship.[146]

Not only was her relationship destroyed by the encroaching war—the plantation on which Emily worked was in the direct path of Mexican soldiers marching to fight General Sam Houston at San Jacinto. The soldiers burned most of the plantation and killed several of its inhabitants, but General Santa Anna discovered Emily and ordered she be saved and held captive.

Anita Richmond Bunkley, author of *Emily, The Yellow Rose*, recreates in her novel the presumed incidents, overtones, and undertones of race that spawned the fame of the Yellow Rose[147] and historians have verified at least some of the incidents surrounding the legend.[148] Emily was said to have been a beautiful woman of mixed African-Caucasian blood, a race that was both legally and popularly referred to at the time as "mulatto," or, in the South, "yellow." While being held captive by Santa Anna, Emily supposedly sent word to

51

General Sam Houston about Santa Anna's whereabouts and then "entertained" Santa Anna as Houston's troops swooped in and captured San Jacinto. The Mexican army was caught completely by surprise, and reports at the time assert that Santa Anna was literally caught "running away from the battle with his studded silk shirt opened and concealed under a dead soldier's blue smock—hurriedly put on during his attempted escape."[149]

Emily survived the battle and made her way to New Washington where Colonel Morgan was residing. Morgan was "so impressed with Emily's heroism that he repealed her indenture and gave her a passport back to New York—the final chapter of which we have no record."[150] The unknown black musician from whom Emily was separated just before the Battle of San Jacinto is said to have composed the song "The Yellow Rose of Texas" sometime just before or after the battle. It was first published in 1858.[151]

Constitution of 1836—The Republic of Texas

The Constitution of the Republic of Texas, also known as the CONSTITUTION OF 1836, was the first Anglo-American constitution to govern the state. Drafted by the convention that had met in March 1836 at Washington-on-the Brazos, and ratified in September of that year, the Constitution of 1836 used large portions of the United States Constitution to create a document that consisted of a preamble, separation of powers among three branches of government (a BICAMERAL LEGISLATURE, a chief executive, and a tiered judicial branch), checks and balances on government power, and a Bill of Rights. Unlike most other state constitutions at the time, no specific limitations and restrictions were placed upon the state government, and unlike the U.S. Constitution, the document gave preference to Anglo-American settlers, the protection of the rights of Anglo people in the unoccupied lands of the republic, and significantly, made specific exemptions of "Africans, the descendants of Africans, and Indians" from state citizenship.[152] The republic's defense of slavery as an institution largely explains why Texas remained independent from the United States for the next nine years since the state, if admitted into the union, would be admitted as a slave state.

The Wild and Wonderful Women of Texas: Angelina Belle Eberly (1798–1860)

ANGELINA EBERLY, a widowed boardinghouse owner in Austin, took on Sam Houston—and won—in the "Archives War" of 1842. Sam Houston often described Austin as "the most unfortunate site on earth for a seat of government," and in 1841 refused to move into the official residence of the President of the Republic of Texas, preferring instead to take a room at a boarding house run by Eberly.

When the Mexican army invaded Texas and took control of San Antonio, Goliad, and Victoria, Sam Houston deemed the City of Austin militarily defenseless, called a special session of the Texas Congress to meet in Houston, and declared the City of Houston the official state capital. In December 1842, after Texas had won its independence from Mexico at the Battle of San Jacinto, Houston ordered his secretary of state to remove the state archives from the City of Austin and transport them to Houston—the new capital of the Republic.

Colonel Thomas Smith, Captain Eli Chandler, and 20 men loaded into wagons traveled to Austin to retrieve and transport the state archives. They entered the City of Austin on January 1, 1843. Upon their arrival in the city limits, Eberly fired a cannon to alert the local townspeople. Heeding Eberly's warning, a vigilante group of Austin citizens descended on the men and chased them to Brushy Creek, just north of Austin. Smith and Chandler were forced to surrender at gunpoint.

The government of Texas did not move back to Austin until 1845, and five years later Austin was officially named the permanent seat of Texas government by a constitutional amendment. During the entire period, 1841–1850, the City of Houston was deemed the capital of the Republic of Texas—but the state archives remained in Austin.[153]

Constitution of 1845—Texas Joins the Union

In 1845, the United States Congress approved a resolution that would bring Texas into the union. President Polk signed the act that made Texas the 28th state in 1845, and the raising of the fifth Texas flag—the flag of the United States—resulted in war. Lasting from 1846–1848, the Mexican-American War ended in a decisive victory for the United States. The signing of the TREATY OF GUADALUPE HIDALGO, along with the GADSDEN PURCHASE OF 1853, resulted in the United States gaining not only Texas but also northern parts of Mexico that would later become part of Arizona and New Mexico, thus allowing the United States a significant land mass upon which to build a southern transcontinental railroad.

On July 4, a convention was called to draft a new state constitution. The CONSTITUTION OF 1845 contained important features such as a bicameral legislature, a governor and lieutenant governor, and a supreme court composed of three judges. The constitution also contained a provision that the state could divide into as many as five states if it chose to do so. The Constitution of 1845 stayed in effect until 1861 when Texas seceded from the union to join the Confederacy. The issue of secession was a very controversial one that divided the state along regional, ethnic, and party lines. TEXAS GEOGRAPHY played a large role in the issue of secession. Cotton was king in the Gulf Coastal Plains of East Texas, and slavery had become a vital institution to the economy of that part of the state. In large sections of the north and west, however, the economy was based primarily on ranching or corn and wheat production, and slavery was virtually nonexistent.[154] Governor Sam Houston, a staunch Unionist, refused to call a special session of the legislature to discuss secession, but a group of influential state political leaders called for a special convention. Lawyers and slaveholders dominated the secession convention, and in 1861 produced the Texas Ordinance of Secession. The convention later reconvened to enact a new constitution to mark the state's membership in the Confederacy. The CONSTITUTION OF 1861, under which Texas joined the Confederacy, was remarkably similar to the Constitution of 1845 with one glaring exception: All references to the United States of America were replaced with references to the Confederate States of America.

Constitution of 1869—The Reconstruction Constitution

When the Union defeated the Confederacy in the Civil War, Texas was required to write a new constitution that would comply with President Andrew Johnson's policy of Reconstruction. The Texas Constitution of 1866, designed to restore relations with the Union, was short-lived and replaced only three years later by a new state constitution after the impeachment of Andrew Johnson and the dominance of the Radical Reconstruction Republicans in the United States Congress. The CONSTITUTION OF 1869, also known as the Reconstruction Constitution, goes a very long way in explaining the complicated system of state government we have today in Texas. We will examine the current Texas constitution and system of government it creates in greater depth in subsequent chapters. However, for now, it is important to keep in mind that the state's current constitution is an extremely long and unwieldy document that creates divisions upon divisions of government power in an attempt to prevent unifications of power such as those the state witnessed under the Constitution of 1869.

The Constitution of 1869 was written to comply with the mandates of the United States Reconstruction Act, passed by the United States Congress after the Union defeated the Confederacy in the Civil War. First, critical changes were made to the Texas executive branch, and the powers of the governor were greatly expanded. EDMUND "E. J." DAVIS, a Reconstruction Republican and former Union general, was named governor of the state. Texans despised Davis, who used the newly expanded powers of the governor to preside over what many perceived to be a corrupt, extravagant administration. Second, Article V of the Constitution of 1869 established a Supreme Court consisting of only three judges appointed by the governor (at the time, Edmund Davis) with the advice and consent of the senate.[155] After Davis was defeated by Richard Coke, a Democrat, in the gubernatorial election of 1873, Davis appealed the election to the Texas Supreme Court. The Court ruled the election illegal[156] and Davis proclaimed his right to finish out his four-year term as governor and barricaded himself in the Texas Capitol. Texas Democrats secured the keys to the second floor of the Capitol and took possession of the building. Coke then summoned the "TRAVIS GUARD AND RIFLES" (a Texas militia named for Alamo defender William B. Travis, organized in 1840 to protect the state);[157] but the Rifles converted from a state guard into a sheriff's posse and instead of protecting Davis protected Coke. Davis then appealed to United States President Ulysses S. Grant, who responded by sending a telegram that stated he would not be sending federal troops to keep Davis in office.[158] The COKE-DAVIS CONTROVERSY ended with E. J. Davis resigning his office on January 19, 1874. Republicans would not hold the Texas governorship for another 104 years.

The Texas Constitution we have today—the Constitution of 1876—was written in direct response to the governorship of E. J. Davis, as well as to the state's experience with reconstruction and as a reflection of our individualistic and traditionalistic political culture. One thing was for certain: The framers of the Texas Constitution were going to make absolutely sure the likes of E. J. Davis would never control the state again.

Understanding Political Culture

All governments and the constitutions that create them reflect the POLITICAL CULTURE of the SOVEREIGN, meaning those that possess the political power in a given country or nation. In DEMOCRATIC GOVERNMENTS, defined as governments ruled by the people, the people are the sovereign that creates and ratifies the constitutions that in turn create the governments under which they live and thrive as citizens.

The United States Constitution reflects the political culture of the citizens of the nation. American political culture is widely understood as containing three primary features: a belief in liberty (limited government), individualism (the individual is central to the group or society), and private property (the idea that individuals—not government—have exclusive ownership of the tangible and intangible goods they gained as a result of their labor or inheritance). The United States Constitution reflects each of these values and beliefs and together comprise the POLITICAL IDEOLOGY of the nation. In order to be legitimate, the Constitution had to embody the values and beliefs upon which the American colonists declared and waged a war of independence against Great Britain. The ideology conveyed in the Declaration of Independence—"life, liberty and the pursuit of happiness"—was a reflection of a larger movement in Western political culture that emphasized reason, scientific method, religious tolerance, and the centrality of the individual over the monarchy and the hierarchy of the church. Thomas Jefferson, the author of the Declaration of Independence, along with John Locke, Thomas Hobbes, Jean-Jacque Rousseau, and Adam Smith, was a major figure of the Enlightenment, also known as the "Age of Reason," and the United States Constitution is a document that fully embraces the 17th and 18th century ideology of the age.

Texas political culture can be understood as an amplification of American political culture. Most political scientists refer to DANIEL J. ELAZAR's typology for describing Texas political culture.[159] Elazar describes political subcultures in the United States as moralistic, individualistic, and traditionalistic, and provides an excellent framework for understanding Texas political culture and, hence, the Texas Constitution. Elazar's description of a moralistic subculture holds that government is a positive force for promoting the "public good or the well-being of the community."[160] While Texas political culture is currently moralistic in terms of embracing social conservativism (meaning generally against abortion, gay marriage, medicinal marijuana, and gun control, and in favor of school prayer), it tends not to reflect the moralistic subculture belief that government is a positive force in achieving a common good. Most Texans are classical republicans in the sense that an ideal government is one that governs least. Limited government is central to Texas political culture and underlies the individualistic and traditionalistic political cultures that mark the state's ideology. As we will see in our study of the current Texas Constitution and Texas government, the Texas Constitution reflects both the past and present state political culture by creating divisions upon divisions of governmental power. Dividing governmental power, as James Madison reminds us in his discussion of the "auxiliary precautions" separation of powers and federalism,[161] limits human inclinations toward ambition and self-interestedness, and preserves liberty. "If men were angels," Madison writes, "no government would be necessary."[162]

Limited government is intertwined with a sense of rugged individualism that pierces TEXAS POLITICAL CULTURE. Individualism holds that government should benefit the individual and therefore (again) be kept to a strict minimum. In Texas political culture, individualism strongly relates to a free market and a sense of capitalist economic expression. The individual, most Texans hold, should be free to express herself or himself in the marketplace, or in the church or statehouse, as she or he sees fit, without government interference. Texans are, indeed, a giving people and in 2013 the state ranked 13th among the 50 states and the District of Columbia in terms of charitable donations.[163] However, Texas political culture holds that giving back to the community or to a person or group is a matter of individual *choice* rather than government dictate about where, or how, or how much they should give. The idea of independent giving is a high priority among Texans; but, the idea of "PUBLIC SERVICE" is not—which helps explain why members of the Texas legislature are among the lowest paid legislators in the country.[164]

The ideological concepts of limited government and a rugged individualism are deeply embedded in the current Texas Constitution of 1876. The history of Texas and the strong historical attachment of Texans to the land helps explain not only the state's political culture but also the Constitution that Texas political culture produced. First, recall that the Constitution of the Republic (1836) gave preference to Anglo-American settlers and protected the rights of Anglo people in the unoccupied lands of the republic. It could be said that Texas itself originated in the strong connections settlers had to the land, and the land-based economy that subsequently evolved. Beginning with the settlement of Austin's Colony from 1821 to 1836 and the growth of an agrarian economy based on slave labor from 1848 to 1860, the state divided along REGIONAL LINES with ranching, corn, and wheat production dominating large sections of the north and west, and "King Cotton" dominating the Gulf Coastal Plains of east and central Texas. Giant cattle ranches in south and west Texas developed a "cowboy culture" in Texas that was marked by fierce individualism, determination, hard work, and independence. Technology also played a part in the land economy of Texas: the invention of barbed wire in the 1870s enabled farmers to protect their lands from grazing cattle; newly designed plows and agricultural equipment allowed farmers to increase productivity; and the building of railroads across the state brought Texas farmers into the national market.[165] But, accompanying the expansion of a land-based economy was a system of land distribution that greatly impacted the politics of the state in late nineteenth and early twentieth centuries. Tenant farming and sharecropping resulted in economic dependency on landowners and landlords by many rural Texans, resulting in the Grange and Populist movements of the era. Cotton as a major commercial good in the state later declined further with infamous boll weevil infestations, the Great Depression, and World War II.[166]

The discovery of oil at SPINDLETOP near Beaumont on January 10, 1901, dramatically transformed the Texas economy and strengthened Texans' attachment not only to the land but to the natural resources it contained. Speculators, entrepreneurs, "wildcatters," and corporate developers flocked to southeast Texas, arriving by the tens of thousands. The LUCAS GUSHER resulted in rapid industrialization of the Gulf Coast with companies now known as ExxonMobil and Texaco developing and building large-scale refineries, pipelines, and export facilities. Extremely close proximity to the Gulf of Mexico along the "Golden Triangle" of Beaumont-Port Arthur-Orange allowed for the expansion of ports that would provide national and international export of oil and gas from the region. Soon after Spindletop, other regions of the state experienced their own oil booms with oil and gas deposits discovered in the Permian Basin in West Texas in 1923 and the "Daisy Bradford No. 3" gusher near Kilgore in 1930. Furthermore, oil and gas discovered on state lands resulted in permanent funds to pay for higher education systems through state royalties, and extreme wealth provided to individuals and families by the discovery of oil and gas on their land spawned a culture of philanthropy that provided funding for the arts, health, education, and historical preservation around the state.[167]

The People of Texas: Demographic Factors that Helped Develop the Texas Constitution, Past and Present

A state land-based economy of ranching, cotton, and wheat production, coupled with land resource economy of oil and gas production, strengthened the bond Anglo-American Texans held to the land that Moses Austin and his son, Stephen, sought to settle. As noted in previous chapters, most of the members of the Old Three Hundred possessed wealth upon arrival, and many brought slaves with them to cultivate the land. The constitutional protection of ownership of both land and slaves in the Texas Constitution of 1836 created an incentive for southerners in the deep south of the U. S. to expand the system of slavery westward into Texas. The number of slaves in Texas rose dramatically from 5,000 in 1830 to over 182,000 by the end of the Civil War.[168] African American populations remain concentrated in East Texas where the southern plantation and sharecropping systems were dominant during the nineteenth century. Also increasing the African American population in East Texas was a huge lumber boom in the 1880s and 1890s. Lumber companies hired many African Americans to work the mills, and blacks comprised 55% of the East Texas sawmill labor force in 1880. Others worked for the railroad stations and freight facilities that transported lumber. In part due to the lumber trade, the African American population of Beaumont increased by 150% from 1860 to 1880, and by 1880, 45% of Beaumont's population was African American.[169]

A "Great Remigration" of African Americans from the North to the South began in the 1970s. The *New York Times* reported in the early 1970s that, for the first time, more blacks were moving *from* the North to the South than vice versa.[170] Many of the migrants are young, college-educated, upwardly mobile black professionals—and older retirees. The 2000 census notes that in the decades 1970–1990, Texas along with other Southern states witnessed large gains in black population. As of 2012, 57% of American blacks lived in the South—the highest percentage in a half-century.[171] Reports indicate that African Americans have begun to return to Texas because taxes tend to be lower than in the North; three of the country's fastest-growing cities in terms of job creation are located in Texas (Austin, San Antonio, and Houston); additionally, housing prices and the cost of living are lower in Texas urban areas than they are in Northern cities.[172] In 2011, Texas had the third largest black population in the country (after New York and Florida), with a large majority of the Texas African American population (about 65%) living in the Houston and Dallas Fort Worth metropolitan areas. Austin, San Antonio, and Beaumont have smaller but still significant black populations.[173] In 2015, African Americans made up 12.5% of the state's population.[174]

During the civil rights movement of the 20th century, Joseph Lockridge of Dallas and Curtis Graves of Houston won seats in the Texas House of Representatives, and BARBARA JORDAN of Houston won a seat in the Texas Senate and was subsequently elected in 1972 to represent Texas in the U. S. House of Representatives (the first African American to represent Texas in the national Congress). Morris Overstreet of Amarillo became the first African American to win a statewide office in Texas (1992, Texas Court of Criminal Appeals), and four African American Texans have represented the state in the U. S. House of Representatives since 1979 (Mickey Leland, Houston, 1979–1989; Craig Washington, Houston, 1989–1995; Shelia Jackson Lee, Houston, 1995–present; and Eddie Bernice Johnson, Dallas, 1993–present).[175] As of 2009, Texas was the only state to have three African Americans serving in statewide office, all Republicans: Texas Supreme Court Chief Justice Wallace Jefferson, Texas Supreme Court Justice Dale Wainwright, and Railroad Chairman Michael Williams.[176] Texas is also home to one of only two black female sheriffs in the United States—Sheriff Zena Stephens (Jefferson County, elected 2016).

The Hispanic population in Texas, mostly of Mexican descent,[177] has fluctuated widely over the course of Texas history. Significant increases in Hispanic migration to Texas occurred in the late 1850s through the 1920s as a result of political and economic instability in Mexico, and again grew from an estimated 700,000 in 1930 to 1,400,000 in 1960. By the end of the 20th century, Hispanics constituted a majority in cities such as San Antonio and El Paso and a sizable minority in Houston, Dallas, Austin, and Fort Worth.[178] In 2015, Hispanics constituted 38.8% of the state's population.[179] By 2003, thirty-eight Hispanics had been elected to statewide office in Texas.[180] In some sections of South Texas, the Gulf Coast, and in the San Antonio area, Hispanics have dominated local politics. They first gained statewide elected or appointed positions in Texas beginning with the elections of Raul Gonzales (1984, Texas Supreme Court); Dan Morales (1990, Attorney General); and Ted Cruz (2012, U. S. Senate). Currently, George P. Bush—who is of Hispanic descent—serves the state as Texas Land Commissioner. In a state where 30% of all registered voters are Hispanic, many political observers both state and national are focused on the "Castro brothers"—U.S. Representative Joaquin Castro and his twin brother, former San Antonio Mayor Julian Castro. Furthermore, a 2014 report from the Office of the State Demographer indicates that Hispanics will outnumber whites in Texas by 2020 and make up the state's majority population by 2042.[181]

Asian Americans constitute less than 4.7% of the Texas

population,[182] but it is projected that the racial/ethnic group will grow at the fastest rate when compared to other racial/ethnic categories in the state.[183] The Asian population in Texas more than doubled between 2005 and 2013,[184] and the state now ranks third in the nation (next to California and New York) in Asian migration.[185] The majority of Asian Americans in Texas are of Chinese, Indian, and Vietnamese descent, with most concentrated in the greater Houston area. Chinese communities are prominent in Houston as are Vietnamese communities in Port Arthur and Korean communities in the Dallas/Fort Worth Metroplex. Five Asian American have served in the Texas House of Representatives: Tom Lee (D-San Antonio-Chinese American); Martha Wong (R-Houston-Chinese American); Angie Chen Button (R-Richardson-Taiwanese American); and two current House members, Herbert Vo (D-Houston-Vietnamese American) and Gene Wu (D-Houston-Chinese American).

At the turn of the 20th century, the United States census counted only 470 Native American Indians in Texas; in 1990, there were 65,877,[186] and in 2010 there were 144,292.[187] The rise in the Native American Indian population from 1900 to 2010 may be attributed to both the cessation of government relocation efforts from Texas and a relatively recent return to Native American culture to the state. The Native American Indian population in Texas rose substantially from the 1950s and until 1980 through a federal government effort to resettle as many as 40,000 Indians in the Dallas-Fort Worth area. Despite the rise in the Native American population, the overall number of Native Americans in Texas is small and the group constitutes only .06% of the overall population of Texas.[188] No member of the Native American population has served or currently serves in any statewide political office.

Texas was relatively trailblazing when compared to other states (especially Southern states) when it came to women's suffrage. Texas was the ninth state in the U.S. and the first state in the South to ratify the 19th amendment (June 28, 1919). And, since 1972, the Texas Constitution has contained an equal rights amendment.[189] Texas is also home to the second female governor in United States history, MIRIAM "MA" FERGUSON.

For the Record: Women's Suffrage in Texas

In 1919, Minnie Fisher Cunningham, president of the Texas Equal Suffrage Association (which became the League of Women Voters), wrote that suffrage passed in Texas due to "intra-party competition, the need for something to trade, and a leader politically shrewd enough to recognize it."[190]

During the 1915 and 1917 legislative sessions, the governor of Texas was James "Pa" Ferguson, an inexorable opponent of woman suffrage. When dissatisfaction with Ferguson's conduct in office grew into a movement to impeach him, the suffragettes and many others rose up against Ferguson, and he was impeached in the summer of 1917.[191] Ferguson's successor, Lieutenant Governor WILLIAM P. HOBBY, was friendly toward woman suffrage and entered into a deal with the suffragettes: If the Texas Equal Suffrage Association would support his candidacy for governor for a full term (he was at the time serving out the remainder of "Pa" Ferguson's unexpired term), he would ensure women the right to vote in the state.

Hobby first pushed for women to gain the right to vote in the state primary—a measure that was adopted by the Democratic Party in 1918. And, when the Texas legislature convened in January 1919, Hobby sent a message recommending that the Texas Constitution be amended to extend full suffrage to women. The amendment passed, and an amazing number of women—386,000—quickly registered to vote.[192] Hobby won the governorship by 80 percent of the total vote.[193]

The following month, June 1919, the federal women's suffrage amendment was submitted to the states. The Texas House convened in special session on June 23 and adopted the resolution, and the Senate quickly followed suit on June 28.[194] The 19th Amendment ensuring women the national constitutional right to vote was formally ratified on August 26, 1920.

Women continued to participate in Texas politics throughout the 20th century. In addition to holding numerous local political offices, some women were also elected and appointed to statewide offices. Dr. Annie Webb Blanton of Austin was elected Superintendent of Public Instruction in 1918, becoming the first woman elected to statewide office in Texas; Edith Wilmans of Dallas became the first woman elected to the Texas legislature (1922); Margie Neal, a Carthage newspaper publisher, was the first woman elected to the Texas Senate (1927); Jane Y. McCallum of Austin was appointed Texas Secretary of State (1927); and Judge Sarah T. Hughes was the first Texas woman appointed to the federal bench (1961).[195]

The TEXAS EQUAL RIGHTS AMENDMENT was first introduced in the Texas Legislature more than a decade before the U. S. Congress passed and submitted to the states the federal ERA, but the first amendment failed to pass the state legislature. A later state equal rights bill, introduced by State Representative Rex Braun (D-Houston) and co-sponsored in the Texas House by FRANCES "SISSY" FARENTHOLD (D-Corpus Christi)[196] and in the Texas Senate by BARBARA JORDAN (D-Austin),[197] cleared the legislature in 1972, and in November, Texas voters approved a Texas Equal Rights Amendment.[198] While a national Equal Rights Amendment to the U. S. Constitution failed to be ratified by the requisite number of states, the state of Texas did vote in favor of its ratification.[199]

The year 1972 proved to be a landmark year for Texas women. In addition to the state ERA being ratified, a number of Texas women were elected to statewide and national office. Barbara Jordan became the first African-American woman from a Southern state to be elected to the U.S. Congress; six women were elected to the Texas legislature (the most ever) with a list that includes two Republican women (Betty Andujar and Kay Bailey), two African-American women (Senfronia Thompson and Eddie Bernice Johnson), and two Anglo-American women (Sarah Weddington and Chris Miller). Democratic state representative "Sissy" Farenthold became the first woman in the nation's history nominated for U. S. vice president, and Republican Anne Armstrong was the first woman of either major party to give a keynote speech at a national party convention. Additionally, 1990 was also a significant year for Texas women. ANN RICHARDS was elected Governor of Texas, and KAY BAILEY HUTCHISON was elected State Treasurer, becoming the first Republican woman elected to statewide office in Texas. Richards, the first female governor to serve the state since Miriam Ferguson, was well-known for her wry wit, feisty demeanor, and independent spirit. She significantly increased the role of minorities and women in state government, added African-American and women to the state law enforcement agency (the Texas Rangers), and improved the Texas prison system. She was defeated in her second bid for governor by George W. Bush in 1994. Hutchison served in the Texas House of Representatives (1972–1976) before being elected State Treasurer, and in 1993 she was elected to the U.S. Senate. Originally elected to fill a two-year unexpired term left vacant by Senator Lloyd M. Bentsen, Jr.,[200] Hutchison continued on to be elected to the Senate in the 1994, 2000, and 2006 elections. Her work in the Senate included strengthening health care benefits for veterans, preventing the federal government from receiving royalties from oil companies drilling on public land, keeping the U. S. government from seizing states' tobacco lawsuit settlements, and maintaining a robust national defense. In 2009, she lost her bid for Texas Governor to Rick Perry and decided not to seek reelection to the Senate. Her seat was filled by tea party candidate Ted Cruz[201] in the election of 2012.

Conclusion

Gaining knowledge about the various constitutions Texas has operated under and the political culture and people that created them provides a foundation for understanding the current Texas Constitution—The Constitution of 1876. Unit 1 has examined the early explorations, settlements, and disputes over Texas land; migration and immigration to the state; and the constitutions of Texas, the state's political culture, and major participants from various race and ethnic backgrounds that have impacted Texas politics. Unit 2 discusses Texas politics in the context of the American federalism and the role of elections, political parties, and interest groups in the state.

Key Terms

Mexican War of Independence
Treaty of Cordoba
Battle of Prueba
Constitution of Coahuila y Tejas
Battle of the Alamo
Battle of San Jacinto

Grito de Delores
Cinco de Mayo
Vicente Guerrero
unicameral legislature
Runaway Scrape
Emily West

Constitution of 1836
Angelina Eberly
Gadsden Purchase of 1853
Texas geography
Constitution of 1869
Travis Guard and Rifles
political culture
democratic government
Daniel J. Elazar
public service
Spindletop—Lucas Gusher
Barbara Jordan
Asian-American migration
women's suffrage movement
William P. Hobby
Frances "Sissy" Farenthold
Kay Bailey Hutchison

bicameral legislature
Treaty of Guadalupe Hidalgo
Constitution of 1845
Constitution of 1861
Edmund "E. J." Davis
Coke-Davis Controversy
sovereign
political ideology
elements of Texas political culture
regional lines
African-American migration
Hispanic demographics
Native-American migration
Miriam "Ma" Ferguson
Texas Equal Rights Amendment
Ann Richards

Unit 2: American Federalism; and Elections, Parties, and Interest Groups in Texas

The first unit of the textbook examined the early explorations, settlements, and disputes over Texas land; migration and immigration to the state; and the constitutions, political culture, and major participants that have impacted Texas government. Unit 2 discusses Texas politics in the context of the American federalism and the role of elections, political parties, and interest groups in the state.

Chapter 4

The American Federal System and Its Significance to Understanding Texas Government

Chapter 4 examines the American system of federalism and explores the powers and structure of local governments in Texas. Upon completing the chapter, you should be able to demonstrate knowledge about:

- Different types of federal systems of government
- Constitutional theories about the United States federal system
- Relevant features of the United States Constitution that pertain to federalism and landmark Supreme Court cases that have shaped American federalism
- The types of intergovernmental grants used in the United States federal system
- The structure and forms of county and municipal governments in Texas

Introduction

A centerpiece of American and Texas political culture is a belief in the concept of limited government. Unit 1 discusses how James Madison's "auxiliary precautions" of separation of powers and checks and balances limit government by dividing power so that no one branch of government (or person or faction) will retain all of the powers of government. Separation of powers charges the legislative branch with the power to make law, the executive branch the power to enforce law, and the judicial branch the power to interpret law. In contrast, AUTHORITARIAN SYSTEMS of government do not embrace the political value of limited government and in such systems one person (usually a dictator) or group of authoritarian agents holds all power to make, enforce, and interpret law. American political culture rejects the political ideology that supports an authoritarian system of government, and the framers of the Constitution sought to ensure limited government by dividing power not only among the branches of government but also among the levels of government. The United States Constitution creates a FEDERAL SYSTEM of government that divides government powers between a central or national government and regional or state governments. The auxiliary precautions of FEDERALISM (the division of power among the levels of government) and separation of powers (the separation of power among the branches of government) ironically provide many Americans cause for both praise for a constitutional system that protects individual rights and limits government and discontent for a system that institutionally creates and promotes government inefficiency.

Federal governmental systems vary in terms of the amount of power and functions they allocate to each level of government. The United Kingdom, for example, has a UNITARY SYSTEM of government in which the central government holds all power, and any powers held by regional governments are those specifically granted to them by the central government. CONFEDERATE SYSTEMS of government, on the other hand, contain an extremely limited central government, and the vast amount of government powers are retained by regional or state governments. The ARTICLES OF CONFEDERATION, the United States' first written constitution, created a CONFEDERAL SYSTEM of government consisting of a national government comprised of a legislative and judicial branch (the Articles did not contain a provision for an executive branch for fear of a monarch) and a loose alliance of states that held almost all governmental power.[202] The events surrounding Shay's Rebellion highlighted the failures of the Articles of Confederation and demonstrated the need for a stronger national government in order to promote a more unified nation, particularly in the areas of currency, foreign policy, taxation, and infrastructure. Ratified in 1788 and instituted in 1789, the nation's new constitution—the longest continuously surviving national constitution in the world—specifically addresses the problems the United States faced under the Articles of Confederation by setting forth in Article I, Section 8, specific ENUMERATED POWERS held by Congress, including the power to coin and

CONNECT ONLINE
ACCESS CODE

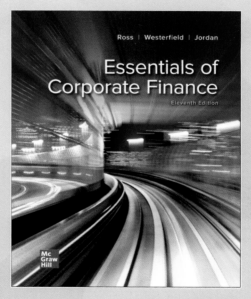

Ross | Westerfield | Jordan

Essentials of
Corporate Finance

Eleventh Edition

McGraw Hill Connect® is your personalized digital learning assistant that makes acing exams, managing time, and getting work done easier—and more convenient—than ever.

Do Not Throw Away

This is your personalized registration code for online access to assignment material.

046870756

5431

TO REGISTER & ACTIVATE, FOLLOW THESE EASY STEPS:

1 Follow the registration instructions provided by your instructor. Register either through your school's Learning Management System or a specific course URL.

2 Click the link to register.

3 Scratch off to reveal the Access Code below— **Do Not Peel**. Enter the code, and click "Redeem".

Scratch here to reveal your access code.
This access code may only be used by the original purchaser.

4 Complete the registration form.

This code is unique and not related to any other registration or ID number. The access code is good for one-time registration. Registration code is valid for the life of this product only. Once this product is out of print, the code is no longer valid and cannot be used.

Need Help?
Visit mhhe.com/support

ISBN: 978-1-265-78839-1
MHID: 1-265-78839-1

EAN

90000

9 781265 788391

01
3431

regulate the value of money, declare war, lay and collect taxes, and regulate trade among the states. In order to further define the American constitutional system of federalism, the TENTH AMENDMENT, ratified in 1791, sought to ensure that, "The powers not delegated to the United States by the Constitution, nor prohibited by it to the States, are reserved to the States respectively, or to the people."

The Tenth Amendment is a cornerstone of the United States federal system of government. In order to understand the meaning and importance of the amendment, it is essential to keep in mind that the United States Constitution was written to create a national government and set forth the powers of the national government. The document does *not* set forth the powers of the state governments. Since the Constitution outlines only the powers of the national government, determining which powers are reserved to the states through the RESERVED POWERS DOCTRINE of the Tenth Amendment requires interpretation of the amendment's phrase "powers *not delegated* to the United States." In other words, a reading of the Tenth Amendment does not directly inform us of the powers the states hold; rather, it informs us of the powers the states *do not* hold, namely those delegated to the national government (such as the enumerated powers to coin money, establish post offices, and declare war).

Constitutional interpretation of the powers not delegated to the national government, and therefore reserved to the states through the reserved powers doctrine, has fluctuated throughout American history. A study of Texas government and the Texas Constitution requires examination of Supreme Court case law as it relates to questions of federalism because of three key features of the United States Constitution: the enumerated powers of Congress (Article I, Section 8), the Supremacy Clause (Article VI), and the Tenth Amendment. This chapter outlines some of the constitutional interpretations, landmark Supreme Court cases, and events that have helped shape American federalism with respect to the powers of the states, and it serves as a companion to student readings and understanding of American government, the United States Constitution, and the powers of the national government. After discussing the powers of the national government and state governments, the chapter concludes with an examination of the structure and powers of local governments in Texas.

Constitutional Interpretation and American Federalism

Major periods of domestic crises in United States history including the Civil War, the New Deal, and the Civil Rights Movement have been marked by the question of whether the national government or the state governments should be primary in the division of government power. The answers to the question have taken a series of twists and turns throughout the nation's history and have inevitably fallen to the courts for constitutional interpretation. Constitutional interpretation of federalism can be defined in terms of two general theories of American federalism—nationalism and states' rights. NATIONAL FEDERALISM holds that the national government is primary in the division of powers, and that the nation is constituted of individuals who come together as individuals (rather than citizens of the states) to produce the nation. States' rights, or COMPACT FEDERALISM, holds that state and local governments are primary in the division of powers, and that the nation is constituted of communities (states) that enter into a constitutional compact in order to maximize their common objectives, such as security against external threat.

The debate between national federalist and compact federalist interpretations of the Constitution is well represented in an extraordinary debate that surrounded the United States Supreme Court decision in *MCCULLOCH V. MARYLAND* (1819).[203] In *McCulloch*, Chief Justice John Marshall combined the NECESSARY AND PROPER CLAUSE (also known as the "elastic clause") of Article I, Section 8, with the SUPREMACY CLAUSE of Article VI to interpret the doctrine of IMPLIED POWERS. The doctrine of implied powers holds that the powers of the national government extend beyond the powers specifically enumerated in Article I, Section 8. Briefly stated, the Supreme Court held in *McCulloch* that although the power to create a national bank was not *explicitly* enumerated in the Constitution, the document did provide Congress the enumerated power to do all things "necessary and proper" to fulfill the enumerated powers (Article I, Section 8). And, since Congress has the enumerated power to coin money and regulate the value of money, it was necessary and proper for Congress to establish a national bank.

For the Record: Early Debates between the Anti-Federalists and the Federalists[204]

One of the earliest expressions of the compact federalist idea in United States history was made by Dr. John Witherspoon, a New Jersey delegate to the Continental Congress who argued before the assembly that the colonies should be considered individuals and that the Congress should be viewed as a collection of colonies. Witherspoon argued that:

> [The colonies] are now collected as individuals making a bargain with each other, and of course had a right to vote as individuals ... That nothing relating to individuals could ever come before Congress; nothing but what would respect the colonies. He distinguished between an incorporating and a federal union ... He expressed his hopes that in the present enlightened state of men's minds we might expect a lasting confederacy if it was founded on fair principles.[205]

There is little doubt but that the constitutional vision embodied in Witherspoon's speech was embraced by a majority of the colonial delegates in writing the nation's first constitution, the Articles of Confederation. The Federalist's call for a new Constitution signified not only the political desire to consolidate the states through a uniform system of laws, currency, and infrastructure to support economic expansion but also an accompanying desire to instill in the people a sense of national unity and allegiance that would lend psychological support to these new national objectives.

The grounds upon which the Anti-Federalists united against the Federalists in opposition to the proposed Constitution was its consolidation of the states and the potential such consolidation held for the destruction of the states. PATRICK HENRY of Virginia, who almost single handedly carried the opposition argument for the first week of the Philadelphia Convention, used his forensic skill and common manner to rally the Anti-Federalists against consolidation.[206] Henry argued at the Philadelphia Convention:

> The fate of ... America may depend on this: Have they said, we the States? Have they made a proposal of compact between the

States? If they had, this would be a confederation: It is otherwise most clearly a consolidated government. The question turns ... on that poor little thing—the expression *We the people*, instead of the States of America.[207]

Henry's emphasis on the practical reasons for rejecting the new Constitution—to prevent consolidation and the destruction of the states—was accompanied by theoretical arguments for rejecting the document. LUTHER MARTIN of Maryland emerged at the Convention as the chief spokesperson for Anti-Federalist constitutional theory. Martin argued that "the people of the continent" were not in a "state of nature" as the proposed Constitution assumed; rather, they had escaped the state of nature by entering into a constitutional compact that had given birth to the respective State governments. These government-creating compacts not only pre-existed the compact under immediate consideration (the United States Constitution) but were still operative. The national Constitution was therefore to be viewed as a creature of the states rather than of individuals independent of their states.[208]

Based largely on the proposed Constitution's failure to embrace the compact theory of government, Martin and other Anti-Federalists attending the Convention refused to sign the document.[209] The objectors were, of course, in the minority, and the United States Constitution was adopted in 1788 by a vote of 63–11.[210]

Since the Tenth Amendment reserves to the states all powers not delegated to the national government, the *McCulloch* decision necessarily limited state powers by interpreting the "delegated" powers of Congress to include the implied powers. The *McCulloch* decision outraged states' rights advocates who viewed Marshall's implied powers doctrine as a blatant and illegitimate encroachment on the powers of the states. The *Richmond Enquirer*, the "preeminent keeper of the states' rights flame," almost immediately began running a series of published attacks on the decision, arguing that the Constitution was adopted by the states, not the people of the states,[211] and that the very life of the Constitution depended upon the existence of state governments.[212] For the first—and only—time in United States' history, a chief justice responded to attacks in the national media. Chief Justice

Marshall published a rebuttal to the attacks in the *Alexandria Gazette* under the pseudonym "A Friend of the Constitution."[213] In his rebuttal, Marshall reiterated his argument in *McCulloch* by writing that the United States "is emphatically and truly a government of the people" and not the states.[214]

While the Court's decision in *McCulloch* expanded powers of Congress through the necessary and proper clause, congressional powers were further expanded in the twentieth century through the Supreme Court's broad interpretation of the COMMERCE CLAUSE. Contained in Article I, Section 8, the commerce clause reads in relevant part that Congress has the power "to regulate commerce with foreign Nations, and among the several States ..." The ability of Congress to regulate interstate trade through the commerce clause was first established in *GIBBONS V. OGDEN* (1824),[215] which held that the power of Congress to regulate interstate commerce included the power to regulate navigation. Volumes of post-*Gibbons* cases demonstrate how the Court further expanded the powers of Congress through the commerce clause, but two cases in particular serve to highlight the Court's general interpretation of the commerce clause in the twentieth century. *NATIONAL LABOR RELATIONS BOARD V. JONES & LAUGHLIN STEEL CORPORATION* (1937)[216] was one of the first cases to uphold an act of the New Deal by ruling that Congress has the power to regulate intrastate activities that have a substantial impact on interstate commerce, and *HEART OF ATLANTA MOTEL V. U. S.* (1964)[217] upheld the Civil Rights Act of 1964 by holding that Congress has the power under the commerce clause to regulate "individual moral behavior" with respect to racial discrimination in public accommodations given the substantial detrimental impact it has on interstate commerce. While *NLRB* and *Heart of Atlanta* embody a national federalist approach to constitutional interpretations of federalism, they also demonstrate COOPERATIVE FEDERALISM in terms of public policy. Under cooperative federalism, the national government retains significant power and the states serve to aid the national government in coordinated efforts to address national problems. Cooperative federalist public policy was pursued by Congress through the New Deal during the Great Depression, and during the civil rights movement and the "Great Society" era of social welfare and social insurance in the 1960s.

The late twentieth century witnessed a shift away from national federalism and cooperative federalism toward NEW FEDERALISM, which seeks to reduce the size and powers of the national government and restore the powers of the states. The shift first occurred in public policy and then in judicial interpretation due in large part to a substantial number of vacancies opening up on the Supreme Court and lower federal courts during the Republican administrations of President Ronald Reagan and President George W. Bush. A states' rights majority voting bloc emerged on the Supreme Court in the 1990s, first surfacing in the area of federalism in the landmark Supreme Court case *U. S. V. LOPEZ* (1995).[218] In *Lopez*, Chief Justice William Rehnquist (a Reagan appointee) joined by Associate Justices O'Connor, Scalia, Kennedy (Reagan appointees), and Thomas (a Bush appointee) declared the federal Gun Free School Zones Act of 1990 unconstitutional on grounds that regulating guns in school zones had no substantial impact on interstate commerce. Two years later, the same majority voting bloc held that the necessary and proper clause did not empower Congress to require local chief law enforcement officers to perform functions required by the Brady Handgun Violence Prevention Act (*PRINTZ V. U.S.*, 1997)[219] and, five years later, ruled that the federal Violence Against Women Act of 1994 had no substantial impact on interstate commerce (*U. S. V. MORRISON*, 2000).[220]

Federalism and Intergovernmental Relations

The new federalism represented in *Lopez*, *Printz*, and *Morrison* was evident in American public policy before the Supreme Court handed down its decisions in the late twentieth and early twenty-first centuries. President Richard Nixon, for example, pushed Congress to create GENERAL REVENUE SHARING programs in the early 1970s in an attempt to restore the power and discretion of the states.[221] And, while President Ronald Reagan terminated general revenue sharing in 1986,[222] he also persuaded Congress to consolidate social welfare programs in order to give state and local governments a greater degree of discretion over how federal welfare funds were used in the states. The national government's use of INTERGOVERNMENTAL GRANTS—the financial transfers from the federal government to support state and local programs—is not unique to new federalism and has been used throughout United States history to entice state and local governments to support and carry out national objectives. Since the Reagan administration, the use of intergovernmental grants has fluctuated with grants for health-related programs growing at a faster rate than non-health related programs.[223] Additionally, since the 9/11 attacks, the national government's use of federal grants has taken on a bi-partisan flair. Democratic President Barack Obama initiated the Affordable Care Act, which created and provided "indefinite appropriations" for the Department of Health and Human Services to award grants to state governments to support the establishment of state-based market exchanges for individuals and small businesses to "shop" for health care coverage.[224] Republican President George W. Bush initiated both "No Child Left Behind," which imposed new requirements and increased funding for state educational systems,[225] and executive orders that created the Office of Faith-Based and Community Initiatives, which allowed religious groups and local religious non-profit organizations to by-pass states altogether and directly receive federal grants to provide social services.[226] Rather than rejecting his predecessor' faith-based initiatives, President Obama actually expanded the program in November 2010.[227]

Generally, intergovernmental grants seek to improve human capital and well-being (through policy areas such as education and health-related service) as well as physical capital (by providing grants to build and maintain road, bridges, buildings, and other infrastructures).[228] Congress determines the types of federal grants to be provided to state and local governments as well as the formulas, award criteria, and conditions and outcomes that might be attached to grants.[229] Congress also determines whether or not grants will include MAINTENANCE-OF-EFFORT (MOE) PROVISIONS, which require state and local governments to match or partially pay for the federally funded program or project with nonfederal state and local funds.[230]

There are two primary categories of grants offered to state and local governments by the federal government. BLOCK GRANTS give state and local government considerable discretion over how the awarded funds are to be spent, and include programs such as community development, TEMPORARY ASSISTANCE TO NEEDY FAMILIES (TANF), and substance abuse treatment. CATEGORICAL GRANTS place more spending constraints on state and local governments by specifying how federal funds are to be spent in specific categories of a program area. Programs such as Head Start programs, Early Learning Initiative programs, and Magnet School programs are examples of categorical grants. Furthermore, categorical grants may be awarded based on the merit of a proposed project or through non-competitive grants provided to all applicant states. PROJECT GRANTS are competitive grants that are limited to a specific project over a fixed period of time. State and local governments have almost no discretion over project grant spending, and the award often carries precise conditions and controls such as demonstrating that students are making adequate progress or ensuring a construction project has successfully passed an environmental assessment.[231] FORMULA GRANTS are non-competitive grants awarded to states based on mathematical formulas designed to ensure fair and equitable distribution of funds by including factors such as state population or the number of students attending public schools in each state. The federal government provided $607 billion in grants to state and local governments in 2011, accounting for 17 percent of federal outlays and a quarter of spending by states and localities. Nearly half of that amount was for Medicaid.[232]

State and Local Governments in Texas

Another complicated layer of government that underlies American federalism is the relationship between state and local governments. In the United States federal system, the power of the state is divided into three spheres: state government, county governments (or parishes in Louisiana and boroughs in Alaska), and local governments (also known as cities or municipalities). The states have historically retained authority over the POLICE POWERS, or traditional government functions, of regulating the safety, health, morals, and education of its citizens. Examples of state police powers include matters concerning the licensing and regulation of the sale of alcoholic beverages; marriage, divorce, adoption, child protection, and probate; public school textbooks and curriculum; the licensing of attorneys and health care practitioners; and vaccination requirement for children enrolling in and attending public schools.

County Governments in Texas

The level of government directly below that of the state is Texas counties. First created as extended "municipalities" under Spanish and Mexican rule, the original local governments of Texas consisted of four major Spanish settlements—San Antonio, Bahia (Goliad), Nacogdoches, and the Rio Grande Valley. After Texas gained independence from Mexico, the state was divided into three "departments"—Bexar, Brazos, and Nacogdoches—and 23 "municipalities" that became counties under the Republic of Texas.[233] The number of Texas counties rose from 36 in 1845 (when Texas joined the Union) to 122 by the time of the Civil War, and 254 by 1931.[234] Today, the number of Texas counties remains at 254.

The structure of county government is outlined in the Texas Constitution of 1876. Since counties are created by the constitution, they serve as functional agents of the state and their powers are limited by specific laws passed by the Texas legislature.[235] The heart of county government in Texas is the COUNTY COMMISSIONERS' COURT. The commissioners' courts consist of four commissioners and one COUNTY JUDGE. County commissioners are elected to four-year staggered terms by the voters residing in designated county precincts. The county judge is elected at-large by the voters of the county to preside over and serve as a voting member of the county commissioners' court. County judges in Texas are not required to hold a law degree since their functions are largely administrative, such as overseeing the election process and presiding over the commissioners' court. And, while officially and constitutionally referred to as "courts," the functions of the commissioners court are primarily administrative rather than judicial. Their statutory and constitutional duties include setting the county tax rate and collecting taxes, building and maintaining county roads, managing the county's fiscal and financial responsibilities, providing for necessary county buildings, dividing the county into precincts, issuing vehicle registrations and transfers, and managing public lands held by the county.[236]

In addition to the county commissioners' court and the county judge, Texas counties have additional elected officers that are charged with overseeing specific county functions. The COUNTY CLERK oversees elections, voting, and official records and documents including birth, death, and marriage certificates. The TAX ASSESSOR-COLLECTOR calculates the amount of property tax that will be charged to property owners; collects taxes including property taxes and sales taxes on automobiles; collects fees for automobile registrations and transfers of title; issues liquor, beer and wine licenses; and registers voters. The COUNTY TREASURER is responsible for depositing all revenue collected by the county, disbursing funds ordered by the county commissioners' court, and maintaining all county financial records. The COUNTY ATTORNEY serves as legal advisor for county government and represents the county in civil and criminal cases. The JUSTICE OF THE PEACE presides over certain civil matters, small claims courts, and misdemeanor criminal offenses punishable by fine only (such as traffic offenses). Finally, the SHERIFF is the chief law enforcement officer of the county and supervisor of county jail and prisons. The sheriff's staff consists of elected precinct CONSTABLES that generally enforce civil laws such as serving subpoenas, seizing property as ordered by a court, executing judgments, and carrying out duties for the justice of the peace courts; and, DEPUTIES who must have law enforcement training and generally assist the sheriff with enforcing criminal law through criminal investigations, arresting suspects, working patrol, and supervising county correctional facilities. The civil/criminal law distinction between constables and deputies has become blurred as Texas counties have grown in population and the duties of the county sheriff have increased. Constables in many Texas counties have been charged with assisting in criminal law enforcement, particularly with respect to traffic codes violations and emergency response.

Texas is also divided into districts that consist of one or more counties. Districts have elected officials charged with performing functions specific to the district. DISTRICT COURT JUDGES preside over state district courts with delegated jurisdiction over criminal law including state felony criminal cases, and civil law such as divorce, adoption, and probate. The DISTRICT CLERK is the official custodian of court documents in cases heard in district courts. The DISTRICT ATTORNEY is the chief prosecuting officer for the district court, represents the state in criminal cases, works with law enforcement to investigate and prepare criminal cases, and determines whether an alleged criminal offense should be brought before the grand jury.

The structure of municipal government in Texas has been significantly impacted by state legislation and constitutional amendments that demonstrate the state's political inclination toward granting local governments a wide degree of discretionary authority. Whereas the structure of county government is outlined by the state Constitution, Texas cities are subject only to statutes, and the state legislature has provided cities far greater freedom over determining the type of government structure they adopt. For this reason, the forms of municipal governments vary across the state.

The first city charter was granted by the Congress of the Republic of Texas to the city of San Augustine in 1837, and the first city charter granted by the newly formed Texas Legislature was to the city of New Braunfels in 1846.[237] The state legislature continued to enact legislative charters establishing Texas cities until 1909, when the state passed a constitutional amendment allowing for the creation of GENERAL LAW CITIES. General law cities are municipalities that are limited to government structures and powers specifically granted by state law,[238] and generally apply to cities with a population of less than 5,000 residents. In 1912, the HOME RULE AMENDMENT was ratified, allowing municipalities of more than 5,000 residents to adopt their own home rule charters and pass ordinances of their own choosing, subject only to the Texas constitution and general laws.[239]

For the Record: Dillon's Rule v. the Cooley Rule

Established in 1868 by Iowa State Supreme Court Chief Justice John Forrest Dillon and quickly adopted by state supreme courts around the nation,[240] DILLON'S RULE holds that local governments including counties and municipalities are creatures of the states and all their powers derive from the state government.

Dillon's Rule was challenged in 1871 by Judge Thomas Cooley of the Michigan Supreme Court. Adopted by Texas and a few other states, the COOLEY RULE held that municipalities possess some inherent rights of local self-government. After the United States Supreme Court upheld Dillon's Rule in 1903 and again in 1923, the states that had adopted the

Cooley Rule were required to abandon the doctrine.[241]

Keep in mind that both Dillon's Rule (1868) and the Cooley Rule (1871) were established before the current Texas Constitution was ratified in 1876, and in many ways the structure of local governments in Texas appear to embrace both doctrines. County governments operate under Dillon's Rule since they are constitutionally creatures of the state and bound by the laws of the state legislature. Likewise, general law cities are bound by the state. However, the Home Rule Amendment clearly embraces the Cooley Rule of inherent local self-government by allowing cities the authority to adopt their own home rule charters, design their own structure of city government, and pass city ordinances of their own choosing.

Ratification of the Home Rule Amendment allowed cities to create their own forms of municipal government. Only three general forms of city government have been adopted by Texas cities: the commission system, the mayor-council system, and the council-manager system. The COMMISSION SYSTEM of city government was once used in Galveston but has now been replaced by the mayor-council form of government.

For the Record: The Commission System of City Government

Created in response to the devastating Galveston Hurricane of 1901 that claimed an estimated 6,000 lives, the commission system was designed as the result of a compromise between the citizens of Galveston, Governor Joseph D. Sayers, and Speaker of the Texas House of Representatives John Nance Garner. The Port of Galveston—at the time the only major port on the Texas Gulf Coast and essential to the cotton economy of the state—had been obliterated by the hurricane, and it was in the state's interest to quickly rebuild.

When the citizens of Galveston approached the Texas legislature for funding to rebuild the city and port, Governor Sayers insisted that funding be provided only on the condition that the state maintain control over the rebuilding effort. The governor then proposed that he be allowed to appoint a five-member commission to oversee the rebuilding of the city and port.[242] The Texas legislature at first rejected Governor Sayers' proposal but ultimately agreed to provide state funds to rebuild Galveston with the assistance of a five-member commission consisting of three members appointed by the governor and two members elected by the voters of Galveston.

The rebuilding of both the City of Galveston and the Port of Galveston was accomplished through the commission system. City commissioners served as both the legislative and executive branch of city government with each commissioner presiding over specific departments essential to the city's rebuilding including water and sewage, roads and bridges, and finance. The system was so successful at rebuilding Galveston that other cities adopted the commission form of city government. In Texas, the cities of Houston, Fort Worth, El Paso, and Greenville soon adopted the plan, and the first city outside of Texas to adopt the commission system was Des Moines, Iowa; followed by Shreveport, Louisiana; Jackson, Mississippi; and Mobile, Alabama.[243]

Criticisms about the commission system's lack of a chief executive, tendency toward internal squabbling, and dilution of minority voting strength brought adoption of the commission system to a halt in the mid-twentieth century.[244] The "father city" of the commission system, Galveston, did away with the system in 1960, replacing it with a council-manager form of government.[245] Today, Portland, Oregon, is the only major United States city that still uses the commission system of government.[246]

The MAYOR-COUNCIL FORM of city government in Texas consists of a mayor and a number of council members or aldermen. The mayor is elected at-large by the city's voters, and the city is divided into wards or aldermanic districts from which the resident voters elect their representative to the city council. The mayor presides at council meetings and is the chief executive officer of the city in his service as head of the police force and budgetary officer of the city. Proposals and appointments made by the mayor are or may be subject to council approval. The city council serves as the chief legislative branch of city government and is responsible for zoning and planning, economic development, city taxes, appropriations, ordinances, and other city functions.[247]

There are two types of mayor-council city governments in the state: the weak mayor form and the strong mayor form. The WEAK MAYOR FORM of city government grants the mayor limited powers over the budget, divides power so that the mayor shares executive and legislative power with other elected city officials and the council, limits the number of terms the mayor can serve, and allows the mayor little or no veto authority.[248] The weak mayor form is used in fewer than 40 Texas home rule cities. The STRONG MAYOR FORM grants the mayor power to appoint and remove department heads, to prepare the city budget for consideration by the council, and to veto council proposals.[249] Many Texas cities, towns, and villages, particularly smaller general law cities, use one of the two types of the mayor-council form of city government. The largest Texas home rule city to adopt the mayor-council form of city government is Houston, which has a strong mayor system with the mayor assisted by a chief city administrator hired by the city council and an elected controller responsible for the city's budget.[250]

The COUNCIL-MANAGER FORM is the most popular system of city government in both the United States and Texas. Currently, 251 of Texas' 290 home rule cities have adopted the council-manager form of government[251] including the cities of San Antonio, Dallas, Fort Worth, El Paso, and Beaumont. Council-manager systems generally consist of an at-large elected mayor who presides over the city council, and other council members elected at-large or by place or district within the city. The mayor and council members are typically low paid, part-time officials who recruit, hire, and pay a full-time, trained professional city manager to run the business of the city.[252] Today, most city managers have graduate degrees in public administration and may be paid as much as $150,000 a year.[253] While city managers are hired, well-trained professionals, they must serve at the pleasure of elected city council members who frequently "pass the buck" on to the city manager when projects and city services do not run according to plan.[254]

Located within the Texas system of federalism are SPECIAL PURPOSE DISTRICTS authorized by state law to provide one or a limited number of functions. Special purpose districts generally have fiscal and administrative authority to operate within their respective spheres. All special districts are governed by a board, but their structures vary widely with some boards elected by the public and most appointed by the states, counties, or municipalities that have joined the district. Their operating revenue derives from a variety of sources ranging from taxes, service charges, grants, special assessments, or a combination of sources.[255] Examples of special districts include school districts, port authorities, water districts, and river authorities.

For the Record: Special Purpose Districts—River Authorities

Texas voters recognized the need to develop and conserve the state's water resources as early as 1917, when a state constitutional amendment was ratified to allow the Texas Legislature to create River Authorities.[256] The BRAZOS RIVER AUTHORITY, created in 1929, was the first state agency in the United States specifically created for the purpose of developing and managing the water resources of an entire river basin.[257]

Today, there are twenty-three river authorities operating in Texas.[258] Among the Texas special district river authorities are the Brazos River Authority, the LOWER NECHES VALLEY AUTHORITY (LNVA), and the TRINITY RIVER AUTHORITY (TRA). Beaumont is home to the main office of the LNVA, created in 1933 to serve the Neches River Basin and the Neches-Trinity Coastal Basin. It operates within Tyler, Hardin, Liberty, Chambers, and Jefferson Counties and serves the watersheds of the Neches River and its tributaries, occupying an area of approximately 10,300 square miles. The river rises near Colfax, Texas, and flows generally southward for a distance of 416 miles before entering the coastal estuary, Sabine Lake, and ultimately into the Gulf of Mexico.[259]

The TRA is a special purpose district that provides conservation and reclamation of water for the reservoir and recreation facilities that are located within a nearly 18,000-square-mile area that comprises the Trinity River basin.[260] The TRA was created in 1955 by an act of the Texas Legislature. Its first Central Regional Wastewater System began operation in 1959 to serve four member cities in the Dallas-Fort Worth area, and in 1969 the TRA completed construction of Lake Livingston Dam to help satisfy water demand for the city of Houston.[261] Today, the special district provides services such as overseeing the recreational area of Wolf Creek Park on Lake Livingston.[262]

Conclusion

Chapter 4 has examined the foundations, theories, and history of American federalism and concentrated on the powers and structures of county and city governments as well as special districts in Texas. Chapter 5 discusses the role of elections, political parties, and interest groups in Texas history and the landscape of Texas politics today.

Key Terms

authoritarian systems

federalism

confederal systems

enumerated powers

reserved powers doctrine

compact federalism

necessary and proper clause

implied powers

Luther Martin

Gibbons v. Ogden

Heart of Atlanta Motel v. U. S.

new federalism

Printz v. U. S.

general revenue sharing

maintenance-of-effort provisions

TANF

project grants

police powers

county judges

county tax assessor-collector

county attorney

county sheriff

county deputies

federal systems

unitary systems

Articles of Confederation

Tenth Amendment

national federalism

McCulloch v. Maryland

supremacy clause

Patrick Henry

commerce clause

NLRB v. Jones & Laughlin Steel

cooperative federalism

U. S. v. Lopez

U. S. v. Morrison

intergovernmental grants

block grants

categorical grants

formula grants

county commissioners courts

county clerk

county treasurer

justice of the peace

county constables

district judge

district clerk

general law cities

Dillon's Rule

commission system

weak mayor form

council-manager form

Brazos River Authority

Trinity River Authority

district attorney

Home Rule Amendment

Cooley Rule

mayor-council form

strong mayor form

special purpose districts

Lower Neches Valley Authority

Chapter 5

Elections, Political Parties, and Lobbying in Texas

Chapter 5 explores the roles and history of elections, political parties, and lobbying in Texas. Upon completing the chapter, you should be able to demonstrate knowledge about:

- ▸ Party structure in Texas
- ▸ The history of parties in Texas
- ▸ One party dominance in Texas
- ▸ The partisan divide in contemporary Texas

Elections are the most common means by which people express themselves in the democratic process. The United States Constitution, with the exception of requirements for holding some national offices, does not set forth the organization and structure of elections. Given the Constitution's silence, the responsibilities associated with conducting elections—even national elections—have historically fallen to state, county, and municipal elections officials and administrators.

The Organization of Elections in Texas

The Texas SECRETARY OF STATE, one of the few official statewide positions filled by gubernatorial appointment in Texas, is the chief election officer of the state. While the Election Division of the Secretary of State's office oversees elections and provides assistance and advice to local election officials on how to properly conduct elections,[263] the vast amount of election-related work in Texas is conducted at the local level. Local ELECTION ADMINISTRATORS are responsible for registering voters, determining voter eligibility, designing ballots and ensuring their accuracy, and selecting and maintaining voting devices. Texas allows early voting three weeks before elections and absentee voting by mail; however, the counting of votes and certification of election results does not occur until the polls close on Election Day.

Political parties play a significant role in Texas elections. All of Texas's 254 counties are divided into precincts or polling places, and voters are assigned precincts and polling places located near their homes. The party's PRECINCT CHAIR is elected for a two-year term during the party's precinct meeting, usually held after the party's primary election in March of even-numbered years. The precinct chair organizes party voters in the precinct, encourages interested party members to register to vote, attempts to increase party member turnout on Election Day, and in some Texas counties serves as an election judge. COUNTY CHAIRS are also elected to two-year terms during the party's primary election. The tasks of county chairs resemble those of precinct chairs only at the county level. They are also responsible in most counties for fundraising and receiving formal filings for candidates to appear on the ballot. County chairs also run their party's primary elections and organize the precinct and county/senate district conventions in order to turn out their party's voters in the general election.[264] Currently, the county chairs of four political parties are listed through the Texas Secretary of State's office: the Democratic Party, the Republican Party, the Libertarian Party, and the Green Party.[265]

The COUNTY EXECUTIVE COMMITTEE is comprised of the county chair and all precinct chairs. The committee works to promote the party's candidates and interests at the county level. The election of each party's STATE EXECUTIVE COMMITTEE occurs at the party's state convention usually held in June of even-numbered election years. Delegates to the state convention convene in meetings based on state senatorial districts (Democrat) or state representative districts (Republican). The district caucuses then select one man and one woman from among their districts to serve on the state executive committee; the entire state convention must ratify their choices. A STATE PARTY CHAIR is then elected to lead the state executive committee and provide state leadership for the party. The state party chair and executive committee are leadership and policy-making positions. In Texas both the Democratic and Republican parties have professional, full-time, paid staff to assist them in performing their duties.

Individuals wanting to become active in Texas party politics must become knowledgeable of the organization of the state's party system and especially the importance of participating in their party's primary. First and foremost, one must register to vote. Voter registration in Texas is administered by county governments but regulated by the state, and Texas state election laws create a closed primary system that for all practical purposes operates as an OPEN PRIMARY SYSTEM. In open primary states, voters must register to vote but they are not required to register with a specific party prior to the primary election. Most voters know the party primary they will be voting in well before they arrive at the polls, but they do not have to make the decision until they actually arrive. Texas is considered a closed primary state only in the sense that once a voter enters the primary of a specific party, he or she may not then go over to vote in another party's primary election. Other states including Arizona, Louisiana, and New York have a fully CLOSED PRIMARY SYSTEM. In a closed primary system, only voters who have registered with a specific party in advance of Election Day may vote in that party's primary. Regardless of whether a state has an open or closed primary system, participation in the primary election is essential to one becoming active in party politics because it is here that voters elect their party's candidates for public office (to run against candidates selected by other parties in the general election) and select the party's precinct chair, county chair, and delegates to the state convention.

Primary voters may not participate in more than one primary election. For this reason, it is not uncommon for less partisan voters to vote in the party primary that features a candidate they feel most strongly about (say, vote in the Democratic primary for a Democratic candidate for county sheriff) and then vote for a candidate they feel is *less likely* to defeat their preferred candidate in another race in the general election (say, a Democratic candidate less likely to defeat the Republican candidate they support for governor). Since voters are free in the general election to vote for any candidate they choose regardless of the candidates' party affiliation, a voter may in the general election cast a vote for both the Democratic candidate for sheriff and the Republican candidate for governor—assuming, of course, both of the voter's preferred candidates won in the primary election.

Texas voters may cast their votes in two different ways. One option is to vote one-by-one for candidates and select candidates from the same political party (STRAIGHT PARTY) or select candidates from different political parties (TICKET SPLITTING). Texas voters also have the option of voting STRAIGHT-TICKET. Straight-ticket voting is simple and requires the voter to merely show up at the polls and punch their party's straight-ticket option at the top of the ballot, thereby casting an automatic vote for all of their party's candidates in every race. Until June 2017, Texas was one of only nine states that allowed automatic straight-ticket voting,[266] and straight-ticket voting was popular in Texas—more than half of all Texas voters took advantage of the option from 1996 to 2017.[267] Because straight-ticket voting requires the voter to have very little knowledge of the candidates and their positions, the option was eliminated in almost every state, and in the 2015 and 2017 Texas legislative sessions became a hotly contested issue in Texas politics. Bills were proposed in both 2015 and 2017 to eliminate the option, and in February 2017 Texas House Speaker Joe Straus, a Republican, made a public call to put an end to the straight-ticket voting option.[268] In June 2017, Governor Abbott signed into law legislation that will end this electoral option in 2020.[269]

An end to straight-ticket voting does not necessarily mean the demise of straight party voting in Texas. The state was a one-party Democratic state before 1952, and has largely been one-party Republican since 1998. The almost half-century in between was a period of ticket splitting beginning with the 1952 and 1956 elections when Texans voted for Democratic Party candidates at the state and local level and the Republican Party presidential candidate, Dwight D. Eisenhower, at the national level. Ticket splitting increased from 1978 until the 1998 general election when Republican Party candidates swept every statewide office in Texas.[270] Straight party and straight-ticket voting became more common in Texas after 1998, and no Democratic candidate since 1998 has held a statewide office.

Political Parties and Interest Groups in Texas

Political parties and interest groups both attempt to influence government. POLITICAL PARTIES seek to influence the operation and control of government by electing its members to important government offices. The goal of political parties is to win elections and thereby control the personnel and operations of government. INTEREST

GROUPS, on the other hand, focus on a specific issue or set of issues in their attempts to influence government by encouraging policymakers to promote their interests through government policies and programs. Interest groups frequently endorse candidates they believe will support their interests when in office, but they do not seek to control the operation of government by directly putting forth political candidates as do political parties.

Raising money is essential to both parties and interest groups. Political parties use CAMPAIGN FINANCE COMMITTEES charged with raising and donating money to the party's political candidates. Campaign funds are used by the party's candidates to advertise their campaign and pay for a staff to assist them in their bids for election or reelection. Interest groups rely on donations from their members and use LOBBYING as a means to gain access to policy makers. Professional lobbyists communicate the views of the interest group to policy makers in an attempt to influence the policy decisions made by elected officials. Interest groups may also bundle their funds with that of other interest groups to create POLITICAL ACTION COMMITTEES (PACS). PACs attempt to influence government by giving money directly to candidates or by engaging in ISSUE ADVOCACY. Issue advocacy involves spending by interest groups, individuals, and corporations to promote a specific campaign issue rather than a particular candidate.

For the Record: A History of the Word "Lobbyist"

The term "lobbyist" was long considered a distinctly American term first used by President Ulysses S. Grant to refer to the throngs of people who daily presented their political requests to him as he enjoyed a brandy and cigar in the lobby of the Willard Hotel in Washington, D.C.

In fact, the term actually first appeared in the *Oxford English Dictionary* in the 1640s to refer to one of the lobbies in the British House of Commons where people could go to speak with their representatives in parliament. The term first appeared in the United States in 1808 in reference to Philadelphia (not Washington) politics, and again in the 1830s in reference to Ohio politics.[271]

Texas is known for its long history of powerful interest groups. Early interest groups were not subject to the formal registration, campaign finance, and ethics laws now required of interest groups. Despite the absence of formal registration, organized special interests in Texas sought to influence and pressure state lawmakers to pass legislation that reflected their interests. The Texas GRANGE, while not formally an interest group as we now understand the term, was a powerful farmers' organization in the late nineteenth century that played important roles both in the Constitutional Convention of 1876 and in encouraging legislators to pass legislation after the constitution was ratified. Much of the Grange-supported legislation still impacts Texas today. Over half of the membership of the constitutional convention were Grangers, and articles in our current state Constitution requiring low salaries for public officers, homestead protection, railway regulation, and restrictions on the state's taxing power are all due to Grange influence on the document.[272] Current Texas laws concerning public education reflect the Grange's strong dedication to improving education in the state including free and uniform textbooks, nine-month school terms, consolidated rural schools, a scholastic age of eighteen, and the availability of vocational courses.[273] Other special interest organizations emerged early in the twentieth century: the Texas Equal Suffrage Association sought to influence state legislation on voting rights; the Texas Christian Temperance Union advocated on behalf of prohibition; and the Southern Lumber Operator's Association fought to get sweeping legislation passed to aide in the development of a booming lumber industry of East Texas.

Industry remained an undeveloped sector of economic life in Texas before 1920. After the discovery of oil at Spindletop near Beaumont in 1901, corporate developers flocked to southeast Texas and with them came the beginnings of modern-day interest groups in Texas. Today, interest groups fall into three broad categories. MEMBERSHIP INTEREST GROUPS are private groups whose members are individual citizens or businesses; NON-MEMBER GROUPS represent individuals, single corporations, businesses, law firms, or freelance lobbies; and GOVERNMENT ORGANIZATIONS represent local governments as well as state and federal agencies.[274] In the 1950s, three new laws were passed in Texas: the Lobby Control Act of 1957, which required lobbyists to register for the first time; an ethics code for state employees, one of a few in the nation; and the Representation before State Agencies Act. One common practice targeted by the laws was payment by interest groups of retainers' fees to legislators.[275]

The Roles and Functions of Political Parties in Texas

James Madison predicted in *Federalist* No. 10 the inevitable formation of FACTIONS, or groups of self-interested individuals who join together to promote their common interests. Factions emerged soon after the American Revolution in the form of the Federalists and the Anti-Federalists who sought to influence the framing of the United States Constitution. Modern political parties surfaced soon after during the critical realigning election of 1800 (featuring Federalist Party candidate John Adams and Democratic-Republican candidate Thomas Jefferson). Since the Civil War, the dominant political parties in the United States have been the Democratic Party and the Republican Party. THIRD PARTIES such as the Populist Party, the Progressive Party, and the Libertarian Party have also played a role in American and Texas politics. While the number of votes for third party candidates in Texas has rarely but occasionally outnumbered votes gained by candidates from the two major parties, third parties have been able to influence politics and government by redirecting political attention toward issues that the dominant parties have ignored, overlooked, or downplayed, especially during times of economic crisis or transition.

Historical examples of third party influences in Texas politics include those of the Greenback Party, the Texas People's Party, Raza Unida, and the Reform Party. Frustrated with the Democratic Party's post-Civil War leadership, the GREENBACK PARTY formed in Texas in response to what its members saw as a growing "cult of the Confederacy" and adherence to a lost cause.[276] Instead of clinging to the past, the Greenbacks sought to focus political attention on pressing social and economic issues such as legal tender, the establishment of a tax-supported education system, and curbing the power of the railroads.[277] The party dissolved after farmers and laborers shifted their allegiances in the 1880s and 1890s to the Texas PEOPLE'S PARTY. The People's Party (or Populists) was an agrarian reform movement that evolved from the Greenback Party, the Grange, and the Farmers'

Alliance. It became the most successful third-party movement in Texas history. The People's Party platform included demands for the preservation of land from large landowners, regulation of transportation, and an increase of the amount of money in circulation. The party became ineffective in the early 1900s largely due to the return of economic prosperity after 1896 and the development of a Democratic Party platform more in line with the interests of farmers and laborers. The People's Party did, however, represent a successful coalition of Anglo small farmers, blacks, and labor that proved important to Texas politics at the turn of the century and instrumental to the rise of other reform groups in Texas in the twentieth century.[278] Other third parties in Texas include Raza Unida (United Party), which actively ran candidates for state office, particularly in the 1970s; the Reform Party, created by Dallas billionaire H. Ross Perot in his presidential bid as an Independent in the election of 1992; and the Libertarian Party, which is currently the largest third party in Texas and the only one to hold an automatic spot on Texas ballots.[279]

Political parties advocate and publicize their positions through a PARTY PLATFORM. A party platform is a formal set of principles and goals generally accepted by the members of the party and presented to the public as a statement of the party's positions and beliefs on political issues. Platforms allow parties to recruit members who share the party's beliefs about how government should be organized and how policy should reflect the party's political, social, and economic agenda. Since the goal of political parties is to win elections, the platform allows parties a foundation upon which to perform the essential functions of recruiting members and candidates, conducting fundraising, and providing campaign support to candidates in order to maximize their success at the polls. Parties need candidates at all levels of government in order to promote their platform, and party organization in the United States is based on the nation's system of federalism. At the local level, party activities most often involve GRASSROOTS EFFORTS and activities led by ordinary citizens who are in close proximity to their neighbors. Closeness allows party members the opportunity to perform important grassroots functions such as holding face-to-face meetings and door-to-door campaigns, organizing social activities, and surveying public opinion about the party and its candidates. Local party members have a say in the functioning of the state party because local members select their party's precinct chair, county chair, and delegates to the state convention. State parties hold state conventions comprised of local delegates that choose the party's delegates to the national nominating conventions and consider resolutions and policy statement that may then be brought forward for consideration at the national party convention. The national party functions as the head of the party, and works to produce a national party platform, unite factions within the party, organize and hold national nominating conventions, and promote the party's agenda on the national stage through social and conventional media.

Texas Political Parties: A History

The history of political parties in Texas can be divided into four major periods: the "politics of personality" (1836–1860); Democratic Party dominance (1872–1952), the era of ticket-splitting (1952–1998); and Republican Party dominance (1998–present).

The Politics of Personality (1836–1860)

There were no political parties in Texas during the Republic of Texas, and the development of politics in the Republic was largely due to populism, personality, and agrarianism.[280] Populism was imported to Texas by Jacksonian Democrats before Texas gained its independence from Mexico.[281] The settlement of Austin's Colony from 1821 to 1836—which occurred at the height of the Jacksonian movement—encouraged individuals interested in land speculation to secure land grants in Texas.[282] Most early Texas settlers were from the Upper South or Lower South where belief in Jacksonian democracy was particularly strong.[283] Jacksonian Democrats were populists who believed in promoting and protecting the good of the common people against government favoritism of corporations and banks that served the interests of the wealthy. Early Texas immigrants were, however, more intent on securing land upon which they could settle and prosper than they were in promoting party identity. The settlers carried with them political beliefs but no true party tradition, and politics in the later Republic of Texas revolved around personalities rather than political parties.[284]

Two personalities dominated Texas politics during the Republic: Sam Houston and Mirabeau B. Lamar. A strong Jacksonian Democrat, Houston served under Jackson in the War of 1812, and his valor earned him the admiration and praise of the future president. After the War of 1812, Houston was elected Governor of Tennessee[285] and thereafter left the state, arrived in Texas in 1832, and accepted an appointment to command a ragtag Texas army against Mexican forces.[286] After the Battle of San Jacinto in 1836, he was elected the first president of the Republic of Texas. The Constitution of the Republic limited the terms of the first president to two years, and no president could be elected to two consecutive terms. Houston was therefore required to step down in 1838, and his popular vice-president, Mirabeau B. Lamar, announced his bid for the presidency.[287]

Lamar stood in sharp contrast to the rugged, heavy drinking war hero Houston. The son of a prominent Georgia planter, Lamar was raised in privilege, classically educated, painted in oils, and wrote poetry.[288] He originally came to Texas to collect historical data and visit his friend, James W. Fannin, but shortly upon arrival decided to stay in the Republic.[289] Houston thought very little of Lamar and his politics, and when Lamar announced his bid to run for the presidency, Houston handpicked two opponents to run against him. Oddly, both candidates—Peter W. Grayson and James Collinsworth—committed suicide before the election, and Lamar became the second President of the Republic of Texas.[290] After serving two terms in office, Lamar was ineligible to run for a third term and Houston was again elected President of the Republic in 1841.

The presidencies of Houston and Lamar stand in as much contrast to one another as do the figures themselves. Houston sought to maintain peaceful relations with Mexico and Native American tribes in Texas, was extremely frugal with state funds, and supported the annexation of Texas. Lamar, on the other hand, was ready to militarily confront Mexico, sought to rid Texas of Native American tribes, was willing to borrow large sums of money to support his efforts, and wanted Texas to remain independent from the United States and expand to the Pacific Ocean.[291] The issue of annexation upon which Houston and Lamar were divided brought about the rise of a new political party in the state. The Texas WHIG PARTY (then known as the American, or Know-Nothing Party) sided with Lamar and strongly opposed annexation, while the Democrats sided with the pro-annexation Houston. After Texas joined the Union in 1845, the Whig Party dissolved and the issue of annexation was replaced with the issue of secession.[292] True to his Jacksonian roots, Houston remained a Democrat and was elected to serve the state as United States senator. While he was away in Washington, Texas politics changed dramatically. First, a new party, the Opposition, or UNIONIST PARTY, emerged. The Unionist Party held strong anti-secessionist sentiment and supported Texas remaining in the Union. Second, the Democratic Party strongly aligned with the secessionist movement. Five of the first seven governors of Texas beginning with James Pinckney Henderson in 1845 were Democrats; however, in 1859, Unionist Party candidates swept the majority of the statewide elections—including the party's candidate for governor, Sam Houston, who had since returned to Texas and declared allegiance to the Unionist Party.[293] The following year, Abraham Lincoln was elected President of the United States. Lincoln's election signaled new calls for secession in Texas and throughout the South, and secession sentiment very quickly reached a crescendo. Against Governor Houston's opposition, a convention for state secession met in January 1861 and voted to secede from the Union. The Texas Unionist Party collapsed and Houston's longstanding reign over Texas politics abruptly came to an end.

For the Record: The Death of Sam Houston

Sam Houston was removed from the Texas governorship after Texas seceded from the Union in 1861, and he returned to his family and friends in Huntsville. His home, The Woodlands, had been sold in 1858 to pay off campaign debts, and for the remainder of his life, Houston was forced to rent a home, the Steamboat House. It is reported he spent his final years grieving not only for Texas and the nation but also for his son, Sam Jr., who was fighting on the side of the Confederacy.[294] Houston died at the Steamboat House on July 27, 1863. His funeral was held in the upstairs quarters of the house.

The *New York Times* reported Houston's "death" a year and a half before Houston actually died. Based on false reports given by its correspondents in the Confederate cities of Galveston and Nashville, an article titled "Death of Gen. Sam Houston" appeared in obituary form after Houston was removed from office but prior to his death. The announcement clearly reflects the southern sentiments of its authors:

> It may be a harsh thing to say, but it is a truth nevertheless, that if old "San Jacinto" had died a year ago his memory would have been cherished by millions and millions of his countrymen, who will now only think of him as one who, after having maintained the flag of his country on many a well-fought field, had not the moral courage to stand by that flag when it most needed his support.[295]

The City of Huntsville and the State of Texas have preserved Houston's legacy. The Steamboat House, originally built in 1858 by Dr. Rufus Bailey, President of Austin College, as a wedding gift for his son, is now a Texas Historic Landmark located in the Sam Houston Memorial Museum Complex in Huntsville.[296] Houston is buried in nearby Oakwood Cemetery in a "self-chosen" site near his friend, Henderson King Yoakum, for which Yoakum County is named. His grave was very simply marked until a new monument was erected in 1911.[297] In 1936, the State of Texas purchased a slab grave marker with an inscription attributed to his longtime friend, Andrew Jackson: "The world will take care of Houston's fame."[298]

Democratic Party Dominance (1872–1952)

The United States Congress and the national Reconstruction Act allowed the Republican Party to control Texas from the end of the Civil War until 1872 when Texas Democrats ousted Republican Governor Edmund J. Davis from office (see Chapter 2). The return of Democratic Party control of Texas for the next century by no means meant Texas Democrats were politically united. While Texas voters remained Democrat on paper, much of the party's post-Civil War history was marked by deep party divisions. At the heart of the Great Depression in the mid-1930s, the politics of economics became the single most divisive issue in state politics and divided the Democratic Party along liberal and conservative lines. Texas Democrats elected to the United States Congress members of the party's liberal faction. John Nance

Garner, J. W. Wright Patman, and Sam Rayburn held significant influence in national politics after the election of Franklin D. Roosevelt, and in state politics, liberal Democratic Governor James Allred attempted to deal with the impact of the Depression by increasing assistance to the elderly, starting a teachers' retirement system, and increasing funding to public schools. The conservative wing of the Texas Democratic Party, with financial support drawn from the state's business and financial leaders, fought to gain control of the state party leadership and propelled W. Lee "Pappy" O'Daniel to the governorship in 1938.[299] The reelection of Franklin Roosevelt to the United States presidency in 1944 heightened tensions between conservative anti-Roosevelt Texas Democrats and liberal pro-Roosevelt New Deal Democrats. Wealthy Texas Democrats with interests in the increasingly powerful oil and gas industry opposed Roosevelt and poured financial contributions into state Democratic candidate campaigns, while liberal New Deal Democrats fought to regain control of the state party's machinery.[300] By the end of the 1940s, the Democratic Party in Texas had clearly split into a conservative wing that held control of state politics and was supported by the state's business, financial, and oil and gas leaders; a liberal wing that supported the New Deal and later championed women's rights, the working class, and ethnic minorities; and a moderate group that shifted back and forth between the two extremes.[301]

Divisions in the Texas Democratic Party are not surprising given the party's complete dominance over state government and politics for almost a century. Southerners in general and Texans in particular had strongly aligned themselves with the Democratic Party even before the Civil War. Opposition to the Republican Party, once seen in the South as the "Yankee" party that freed the slaves and forced Reconstruction, was passed along to subsequent generations often without question or reflection. And, as the national Democratic Party moved further and further away from old South views on civil rights and social programs, many Texans still refused to vote Republican.[302] The term "YELLOW DOG DEMOCRAT," which derives from the saying, "I'd vote for a yellow dog if he ran on the Democratic ticket," became common in the South in the early twentieth century to describe Democrats who were so loyal to the party they would vote for Democratic candidates even if they disliked their views and political positions.[303] The term later came to refer to

Democrats who held more moderate to conservative views, particularly in terms of economic policy.

An Era of Ticket-Splitting (1952–1998)

The move away from Democratic Party dominance toward ticket-splitting in the South occurred very gradually as outdated Civil War labels lost their meaning in the electorate and the Republican Party reconstructed its platform to lure economically and socially conservative Southerners into its ranks. In Texas, the era of ticket-splitting began in 1952. Conservative Democrat Governor R. Allan Shivers, elected in 1949, took control of the party machinery by instituting a purge of the State Democratic Executive Committee and stacking its membership with his supporters. Shivers also engineered a change in the state's election laws to permit candidates to cross-file in both the Democratic primary and the Republican primary in the 1952 presidential election. As a result, conservative Democrats, termed "Shivercrats," filed in both primaries, thereby enabling them to vote for Democrats at the local level and the Republican presidential candidate, Dwight D. Eisenhower, at the national level.[304] Eisenhower's victory in Texas, strongly garnered by Shivers' change in state election laws, compelled the liberal wing of the Texas Democratic Party to focus its attention on unseating Shivers and his supporters. Liberal Texas Democrats fought to regain power in the state and, in the nation's capital, Speaker of the House Sam Rayburn and Senate Majority Leader Lyndon Johnson, both Texans, battled Shivers for control of the state Democratic Party. Ralph Yarborough, endorsed by the liberal wing of the party including labor and a number of women activists, unsuccessfully challenged Shivers in the 1952 Democratic primary. When Yarborough again lost the governor's race in 1956 to conservative Democrat Marion Price Daniel, Sr. in a close run-off campaign, Yarborough threw his hat in the ring to gain Daniel's vacated seat in the United States Senate. Texans clearly split their tickets in the 1956 primary election: President Eisenhower, again with Shiver's help, carried the state, and Yarborough squeaked through the primary to join Lyndon Johnson as the second sitting United States Senator from Texas.[305]

The campaign and ultimate election of President John F.

Kennedy and his vice presidential running mate, Lyndon Johnson, dominated state politics in the early 1960s. Conservative Democrats retained control of the state convention, but the Kennedy/Johnson ticket carried Texas in 1960 and reversed the direction of the 1952 and 1956 presidential elections. Despite the 1960 presidential victory for Texas Democrats, the party was dealt a major blow in the runoff election to fill the United States Senate seat left vacant by Vice President Johnson. JOHN G. TOWER, the only viable Republican candidate in the race, defeated conservative Democrat William A. Blakley, who had been appointed to fill Johnson's Senate seat until an election could be held. Tower's victory was seen by some to be an electoral fluke and others to be the beginning of two-party politics in Texas. Hindsight demonstrates the latter to be correct. The first Republican elected to statewide office since Reconstruction, Tower was re-elected to the United States Senate in 1966, 1972, and 1978.[306] His years in the Senate allowed him to connect the Texas Republican Party to the national party, and the state party to local Republican candidates.[307] Tower's electoral success caused the Democratic Party membership to rally around John Connally, a moderate to conservative Democrat, in his successful run for Texas Governor in 1962.[308]

The Kennedy assassination on November 22, 1963, traumatized the citizens of Texas and deeply shook the state Democratic Party. President Johnson easily won the Texas vote in the 1964 presidential race, but four years later Democratic presidential candidate Hubert Humphrey barely managed to carry the state in the presidential election.[309] Johnson's ascendancy to the presidency, Governor Connally's iron rule of the state Democratic Executive Committee, and pressing issues of civil rights served to align moderate and liberal Texas Democrats against the more conservative Democratic forces in the state.

The party's longstanding resolution that only whites were allowed to vote in the Texas Democratic primary had been struck down by the United States Supreme Court in 1944 in the case of *SMITH V. ALLWRIGHT*.[310] Previous courts had held that the Democratic Party was a "voluntary association" that could prescribe its own membership rules; but, in *Smith* the Court ruled that parties were agents of the state and excluding people from membership in the party based on race was a violation of the United States Constitution. After the *Smith* decision, the conservative state party leadership stepped up its use of the POLL TAX in an attempt to deter black voters from participating in primary elections. Codified into Texas law through a state constitutional amendment in 1902, the poll tax was a method to prevent economically disadvantaged citizens from voting in the party's primary. In Texas, local chapters of the League of Women Voters and religious and political leaders fought diligently against the state tax[311] and were able to get a proposition to repeal the state poll tax on the November 9, 1963, ballot. The proposition failed.[312] The following year, the 24TH AMENDMENT to the United States Constitution was ratified prohibiting poll taxes in federal elections. The 24th Amendment was quickly followed by the passage of the Voting Rights Act of 1965, signed into law by President Lyndon Johnson, and the Supreme Court's ruling in 1966 that state poll taxes violated the Equal Protection Clause of the 14th Amendment.[313]

For the Record: Congressman Jack Brooks

One of the leading Texas Democrats in Washington on the issue of civil rights was Congressman Jack Brooks. Brooks was elected to represent Jefferson County in the Texas Legislature in 1946. He later represented the Second Congressional District in the United States House of Representatives from 1953 through 1966, and the Ninth Congressional District from 1967 to 1995. He served in the United States Congress for 42 years.

Brooks rose in Congress under the tutelage of Speaker Sam Rayburn and Senator and President Lyndon Johnson. He helped write the Civil Rights Act of 1964 and the Voting Rights Act of 1965, and he was one of only a handful of southern congressmen to support civil rights legislation.[314] He refused to sign the notorious "Southern Manifesto," signed by 100 members of Congress, opposing school desegregation after the Supreme Court's decision in *Brown v. Board of Education* (1954). Later in his career, Congressman Brooks sponsored both the Americans with Disabilities Act of 1990 and the Civil Rights Act of 1991. He died in Beaumont in 2012 at the age of 89.

The 1972 general election demonstrated a rising trend among Texas voters to split their tickets between Democratic candidates and Republican candidates. Democrats held control of state and local offices; however, Republican presidential candidate Richard M. Nixon gained a whopping 60.20% of the Texas vote against Democratic candidate George McGovern.[315] Furthermore, the narrow margin of Democratic victories in state races indicated the Republican Party was gaining ground in the state. The 1972 election occurred in the wake of the SHARPSTOWN STOCK-FRAUD SCANDAL, which centered on charges that state officials had made profitable bank-financed stock purchases in return for passing legislation desired by the financier, Houston businessman Frank W. Sharp. By the time the smoke cleared, a number of state Democratic officials had been charged with numerous other offenses including nepotism and the use of state-owned funds to buy a pickup truck.[316] The Sharpstown Scandal marked the end of the political careers of Texas House Speaker Gus Mutscher, Governor Preston Smith, and Lieutenant Governor Ben Barnes, all of whom were closely tied to the old Democratic establishment.[317]

For the Record: The "Dirty Thirty"

The "DIRTY THIRTY" was a bipartisan group of Texas legislators that pressed for an investigation of the Sharpstown Stock-Fraud Scandal. Texas Speaker of the House Gus Mutscher, who had been named in the scandal, retaliated against the "Dirty Thirty" by blocking legislation introduced by the group's members.[318] Despite Mutscher's attacks, members of the group including Democrats Bill Bass, Price Daniel, Jr., and John Hannah, and Republicans William J. Blythe, Jr., Tom Craddick, and Jim Earthman,[319] continued to press for an investigation.

In the end, the "Dirty Thirty" prevailed. In addition to the political demise of Speaker Mutscher, Governor Smith, and Lieutenant Governor Barnes, far-reaching campaign finance reform legislation was passed in Texas,[320] and a new group of Texas Democratic Party leaders emerged. Over half of the members of the Texas legislature were replaced in the 1972 election, and electoral victories by Democratic Party reform candidates such as William P. Hobby, Jr. as Lieutenant

Governor and John Hill as Attorney General demonstrated the party's changing direction. Frances "Sissy" Farenthold, backed by college students and liberals, emerged as the liberal Democratic gubernatorial frontrunner against conservative Democratic rancher-banker Dolph Briscoe. Briscoe was able to split the liberal coalition by securing the neutrality of organized labor, and won the election.[321]

The following year, Texas voters demonstrated that their confidence in the legislature had been somewhat restored by their approval of a constitutional amendment that allowed the legislature to sit as a constitutional convention.[322] The TEXAS CONSTITUTIONAL CONVENTION OF 1974 failed by three votes to approve a proposed new constitution for Texas voters to consider.

Texas Republicans proved they could successfully challenge Democrats for control of state politics when WILLIAM "BILL" CLEMENTS won the governor's race in 1978. Clements' victory as the first Republican Governor of Texas since Reconstruction was due in part to a split in the Texas Democratic Party after Attorney General John Hill, Jr. defeated the incumbent governor, Dolph Briscoe, Jr. in the Democratic primary. The Briscoe children and other Briscoe supporters endorsed Clements, who won by a narrow margin.[323] But Democrats could no longer turn a blind eye to the growing strength of the Republican Party in Texas, especially after Republican presidential candidate Ronald Reagan and his Texan vice presidential running mate, George H. W. Bush, soundly carried Texas in the 1980 election. Texas Democrats regrouped. Aided by the war chests of incumbent United States Senator Lloyd Bentsen and incumbent Lieutenant Governor William P. Hobby, Jr., the party put forward a new slate of Democratic challengers for the 1982 statewide elections that included Mark White for governor, Jim Mattox for attorney general, and Ann Richards for state treasurer.[324] All of the statewide Democratic candidates won at the polls, including Mark White, who defeated incumbent Governor Clements. Clements rebounded to successfully defeat White in the 1986 gubernatorial election, thereby becoming one of only three Texas governors to serve non-consecutive terms.[325] And, incumbent United States President Reagan again carried the Texas presidential vote in

1984. A new term, "BLUE DOG DEMOCRATS," emerged to describe Democrats who had crossed over party lines and voted for Reagan and his policies in the 1980s.[326] Instead of being blinded by party loyalty like "yellow dogs," the self-proclaimed "blue dogs" complained they had been "choked blue" by their own party.[327] Furthermore, Democrat Phil Gramm, elected in 1978 to serve in the United States House of Representatives, led a group of House Democrats called "boll weevils" in support of President Reagan's wide-ranging budget and tax cut plans.[328] After the Democratic leadership stripped him of his seat on the House Budget Committee, Gramm switched to the Republican Party, won his House seat, and went on to defeat moderate Texas Democrat Lloyd Doggett in 1984 for the United States Senate seat left vacant by retiring Republican United States Senator John Tower.[329]

The 1990s was a decade of rapid growth for the Texas Republican Party. Members of the Republican Party held about 1/3 of the seats in both chambers of the Texas legislature by the time Democrat ANN RICHARDS was elected governor in 1990.[330] Two years later, the number of Democrats voting in the Democratic primary in Texas decreased from 1.8 million to 1.5 million, and the number of Texas legislative seats held by Republicans rose to 59 (out of 150) in the Texas House, and 13 (out of 31) in the Texas Senate.[331] In 1993, Republican KAY BAILEY HUTCHISON secured the second Senate seat from Texas, making her the first woman elected to the United States Senate from Texas, and the following year, Republican George W. Bush defeated Richards in the gubernatorial election. The 1994 election also saw Texas Republicans gain all three seats on the state Railroad Commission and pick up two congressional seats. Additionally, one time Democrat-turned-Republican Rick Perry retained his office as Agricultural Commissioner.[332] The end of the era of Democratic Party dominance of Texas politics appeared inevitable.

The Era of Republican Party Dominance (1998–present)

The decade of the 1990s was one of Republican Party rise and dominance over Texas government and politics. GEORGE W. BUSH's gubernatorial victory over popular incumbent Ann Richards in the 1994 election marked the second time a Republican held the governor's office since Reconstruction. The party won control of the Texas Senate by a slim majority (17 of 31 seats) in 1996, and two years later won all 27 statewide offices. The 2000 elections demonstrated the continuing rise in Republican votes in Texas with former Governor George W. Bush overwhelmingly gaining the state's vote for President of the United States, and Michael Williams, a Bush appointee to the Texas Railroad Commission, winning his first full term on the commission. In 2002, the Republican Party won control of the Texas House, making TOM CRADDICK the first Republican Speaker since Reconstruction,[333] and giving Texas Republicans control over a UNIFIED GOVERNMENT. Unified government is a political situation in which both chambers of the state legislature as well as the governorship are controlled by members of the same party. It allows the party in control to more easily pass laws that fit their legislative agenda, since potential opposition by minority party members in the legislature diminishes due to sheer number of votes. It also reduces the likelihood that a veto by the governor will be overridden by a legislative majority that holds membership in the governor's political party.

Districting and redistricting are also important factors in the era of Republican Party dominance in Texas. Since the number of seats each state gets to the United States House of Representatives is based on population, the United States Congress after every ten-year national census apportions to each state the number of seats each state will get in the United States House of Representatives. After apportionment is performed by the national Congress, state legislatures have the responsibility of dividing the states into national congressional districts as well as into relevant state districts. The Texas House passed a bill in 2001 to draw new districts for the state House and, after the Texas Senate rejected the bill, the House assigned the task of REDISTRICTING to the Legislative Redistricting Board (LRB). The LRB drew new congressional districts clearly to favor Republican candidates. Despite intense objection, the LRB voted to use their new redistricting map in the statewide election of 2002, which resulted in a Republican majority of 88–62 in the Texas House of Representatives (compared to a 72–78 minority prior to the 2002 election).[334]

Texas Lieutenant Governor RICK PERRY assumed the governorship of Texas when Governor George W. Bush was elected President of the United States in 2001. His ascendancy to the governorship would begin a historical record of Perry being the longest serving governor in Texas history—a period stretching continuously from 2001 until 2015. Since Texas does not have term limits for statewide offices (as discussed in Chapter 8), Perry was technically able to serve as governor for as long as the voters continued to reelect him, but he chose not to seek reelection in 2014 after 14 years in the position. In his first term as governor, Perry did not have Republican majorities in both chambers of the Texas Legislature and had to use his gubernatorial power of veto to advance his legislative agenda. At the conclusion of the 2001 legislative term, Perry vetoed 79 bills in one day, commonly referred to as the FATHER'S DAY MASSACRE.[335] The fact that Perry waited until the conclusion of the legislative session to veto the bills is significant because the veto of bills passed after the legislative session has ended is not subject to an override vote except with a call by the governor for a special session (as discussed in Chapters 6 and 7). Governor Perry was not going to call a special session specifically to address the possibility of overriding one of his vetoes. While Perry's use of the power of veto was needed early in his governorship in order for him to advance his legislative agenda, it was no longer required after the Republican Party gained control of both the Texas House and Texas Senate in 2003. Republican Party control of both houses of the Texas legislature allowed Republican legislators to enact into state law a conservative political agenda that included some proposals to benefit the business community and others designed to please social conservatives. Texas Republicans aggressively pushed for more lenient rules regarding intrastate commerce, steadfastly defended the state's low-tax ethos, fought for additional state restrictions on abortion, and enacted more lenient laws concerning firearm ownership and carry.

The legacy of Republicans dominating Texas for roughly the past two decades has included a strategy referred to as the "TEXAS MODEL." Due in part to Governor Perry's run for the United State presidency, *USA Today* ran a column entitled "Rick Perry: Follow the Texas Model of Success," in which the governor addressed the creation of opportunity in Texas. Perry wrote the article in which he asserted Texas "maintain[s] low taxes, smart regulations and fair courts." He also said the state has "created three out of every 10 jobs in America over the last 10 years."[336] Readers may agree or disagree with Perry's policies regarding the regulation of the economy, but statistics demonstrate the relative success of the Texas Model advanced by Perry during his terms as governor. Employment in Texas grew by over 2.2 million between December 2000 and January 2015, an increase of almost twenty five percent.[337]

After January 2015, employment in Texas began to decline. In March 2015, Texas lost 25,000 jobs across all sectors,[338] and falling oil prices were linked to a loss of 8,300 Texas oil industry jobs in April 2015.[339] Oil traded for over $100 per barrel in 2014 but was down to $60 per barrel in May and June 2015,[340] and by mid-December 2015 the price of Brent crude as well as West Texas Intermediate trading was between $30 and $40 per barrel.[341] On May 16, 2017, both measures of crude prices were near $50 a barrel.[342] The downward trend in oil prices has been a source of concern about Texas; however, fossil fuel industries were the source of less than 4% of Texas nonagricultural jobs in 2011.[343] Also related to the state of the Texas job market is the issue of health insurance. In 2010, one quarter of Texans did not have health insurance, and in 2015 the Centers for Disease Control and Prevention reported that 16.8% of Texans were without health insurance—the largest percentage of the population without health insurance than any other state in the union.[344] Furthermore, job creation in Texas has only matched population growth, so there is little pressure or incentive to pay higher wages.[345] Whether the Texas Model is ideal for other states to follow is still a subject appropriate for debate, and readers can draw their own conclusions about it. However, it is undeniable this will be part of Rick Perry's legacy, whether history judges it positively or negatively.

The "Texas Model" is part of the legacy of the Republicans controlling Texas for most of the past two decades. This style of governing includes positions on issues that are consistent with those of business interests and is promoted as something that is good for the business community. However, in recent years the business community has come into conflict with the Republican Party in Texas. The Texas Association of Business is the biggest business organization in Texas and represents over 4,300 employers. It has a history of lobbying for reduced regulation and taxation and helped Republicans win control of Texas. Republican primary voters now decide who wins most major elections in Texas and connect more with appeals based on cultural conservatism than those grounded in arguments about what is good for business. Lieutenant Governor Dan Patrick advocated for a bill that would force Texans to select the public restrooms they used based on their birth sexes when in public buildings. Transgender Texans would not be allowed to use restrooms that matched their gender identities in public buildings if this law passed.[346] The President of the Texas Association of Business asserted, "Discriminatory legislation is bad for business," when explaining his opposition to this bill.[347] Many corporations joined a coalition assembled by TAB to oppose the bill, including Amazon, Google, Dell, and Apple among others.[348] While Republicans are likely to control the state throughout the near future, one dominant party in Texas does not mean one position on every issue among Texans. The discussion of other controversies below will illustrate this observation as well.

Legislative Issues during the Era of Republican Party Dominance

Among the many political issues addressed by the Texas legislature during the era of Republican dominance and the Perry administration were ABORTION and gun rights. The national Republican Party platform opposes abortion and generally Texas Republicans are no exception. Prior to the United States Supreme Court case of *Roe v. Wade* (1973),[349] abortion was not uniformly legal or illegal across the United States; however, access to abortion could be limited or permitted by state law. The *Roe* decision held that women have a constitutional right to privacy that extends to the right of a woman to terminate her pregnancy through an abortion. States may not, therefore, pass laws that ban abortion outright. But, after the Court's decision in *Planned Parenthood v. Casey* (1992),[350] states may pass laws that regulate or restrict the procedure. *Roe v. Wade* is unlikely to be reversed in the near future, and state legislators and governmental officials who want to restrict abortion must do so in accordance with the limited authority they have based on the *Roe* and *Casey* decisions. Texas Republicans have worked within the guidelines set forth by the United States Supreme Court to enact legislation to limit access to abortion and increase the procedural steps required to obtain an abortion. Near the end of Rick Perry's governorship, the Texas Legislature was successful in passing a series of new laws restricting abortion in the state.

Republicans achieved a 2/3 SUPERMAJORITY in the Texas House

of Representatives in 2010. Achieving a supermajority allowed Republican members to dominate the processes and agenda of the chamber[351] (for reasons that will be discussed in Chapter 6). In January 2011, Governor Perry aggressively promoted a bill mandating that women who choose to have an abortion must undergo an ultrasound twenty-four hours prior to the abortion procedure.[352] The reason for the ultrasound bill, according to the bill's sponsor, Sid Miller, was that the legislature wanted "to make sure she knows what she is doing."[353] The bill passed the Texas House 107–42 and Perry signed it into law.[354] Another abortion bill, HOUSE BILL 2, was passed in 2013. State Senator Wendy Davis, a Fort Worth Democrat, filibustered the bill during that year's first special session, but the legislature approved it in a second special session.[355] The law banned abortions once gestation had continued for more than twenty weeks and included new rules for administering RU-486 (a drug that induces abortions).[356] It also required that abortion providers maintain admission privileges at hospitals in their area, and that facilities providing abortions meet the same standards required of ambulatory surgical centers.[357] Before the passage of House Bill 2, forty abortion providers made their services available in Texas, but most clinics performing abortions closed after the bill was enacted.[358] In June 2016, the United States Supreme Court invalidated the sections of the Texas law that required abortion providers to maintain admitting privileges and facilities to meet standards identical to ambulatory surgical centers, citing the undue burden the requirements placed on those seeking to obtain an abortion.[359] A few clinics have reopened since the Supreme Court's ruling, including clinics in Dallas,[360] Austin,[361] and Waco,[362] but the numbers are still far behind the number of clinics in Texas prior to House Bill 2.

Gun rights have also been high on the state legislative agenda during the era of Republican dominance. The Second Amendment to the United States Constitution states: "A well-regulated militia being necessary to the security of a free state, the right of the people to keep and bear arms shall not be infringed." The Second Amendment was used by the Supreme Court to strike down a local gun control ordinance in *D.C. v. Heller* (2008)[363] and again in *McDonald v. Chicago* (2010).[364] The *McDonald* case differed from the *Heller* case in that Washington, D. C. is not a state and therefore not subject to the 14th Amendment.

Chicago is a city within a state and was created and given its authority by the state of Illinois (see our discussion of Dillon's Rule in Chapter 4). Like all of the rights in the Bill of Rights, the Second Amendment originally applied only to the national government (see *Barron v. Baltimore*, 1833),[365] but the *McDonald* case incorporated the Second Amendment to apply to the states. Moreover, the Texas Constitution contains a state constitutional provision that protects the rights of Texans to keep and bear arms.[366]

The history of the right to bear arms in Texas has relevance in contemporary discussions of the topic. The Texas legislature is empowered by the state constitution to pass laws restricting weapons. In 1871, during the era of Reconstruction, the Texas legislature passed a law making it illegal to carry a pistol outside of one's home. The law was not repealed during the era of Democratic Party dominance in Texas[367] and remained on the books for over 120 years.[368] Governor George W. Bush openly supported a concealed-weapons bill during his first gubernatorial campaign in 1994,[369] and after taking office signed the concealed carry bill into law.[370] Republicans in favor of gun rights were able to pass legislation extending the right to keep and bear arms after the party gained a majority in the state legislature, and in the past twenty years Texas has become more and more lenient with regard to carrying firearms. The first regular legislative session held after the election of current Texas Governor Gregg Abbott in 2014 resulted in the governor's signing into law a bill allowing CAMPUS CARRY.[371] Campus carry allows individuals with the appropriate licenses to bring concealed handguns on public college and university campuses.[372] During the same 2015 session, the state legislature passed an OPEN CARRY bill which allows licensed Texans to openly carry handguns. The bill was supported by only five Democratic members of the House (by a vote of 102–43), and no Democratic members of the Senate (by a vote of 20–11).[373] In a public show of his support for the bill, Governor Abbott signed the bill into law at a shooting range and gun store in Pflugerville.[374] The governor also signed into law a gun-related bill passed during the 2017 regular legislative session. The law reduced the first-time firearm permit fee from $140 to $40 and the five-year permit renewal fee from $70 to $40. While the state will forego roughly $22 million of revenue in the next budget cycle because of permit fee reductions, the National Rifle Association reports that Texas now has the lowest fees of this type of any state.[375]

Groups with a strong interest in these policies have been vocal about gun rights in Texas politics over the past several years. Open Carry Texas supports the legalization of openly carrying pistols without licenses; the president of that organization has called these licenses a "second amendment tax."[376] Chapters of Open Carry Texas have also posted videos on the web showing themselves entering restaurants with rifles on their backs.[377] In 2014 the NRA (National Rifle Association) characterized these events as bizarre and claimed they worked against the goals of the gun rights movement on one of its blogs.[378] Chris Cox, a high-level official within the NRA, publicly blamed "the staffer who wrote that piece and expressed his personal opinion" shortly thereafter on their website.[379] Open Carry Texas had stopped openly displaying their weapons inside businesses and other public venues weeks before the controversy, according to C. J. Grisham, who was their president at the time.[380] Further, as *Texas Monthly* pointed out in April 2015, multiple organizations openly carried long guns into public places to highlight inconsistencies in state law that existed at that time. In that era, anyone could carry long guns openly in public places with no permit requirement, but handguns had to be concealed and carried by licensed Texans.[381]

The National Rifle Association is an extremely influential organization and its name is associated with dedicated gun rights advocacy in national discourse. Such a dispute might be assumed to slow down a more state-centric organization like Open Carry Texas, but they have remained active on these issues. However, during this controversy they were meeting with lawmakers, and Grisham was extremely confident openly carrying pistols would be legalized in 2015.[382] As observers of Texas politics now know, Governor Abbott signed a bill permitting licensed Texans to openly carry handguns in June 2015.[383] In 2017 the Texas Legislature considered whether to allow those who legally own firearms to carry their pistols (in holsters or concealed) without a license from the state. Officials speaking for the Combined Law Enforcement Associations of Texas asserted this law would make it more difficult for police officers to carry out their duties.[384] C. J. Grisham said law enforcement interests had predicted pervasive problems with concealed carry and open carry. He asserted, "They have zero credibility. They've been wrong every time."[385]

Whether Grisham and Open Carry Texas win future debates over gun rights will be of interest to millions of Texans. In recent years he and those with similar beliefs have had much success in Texas politics and they are likely to continue to advocate for a more lenient approach to gun policy in Texas.

The Partisan Divide and the State of Texas Politics Today

Republicans have remained dominant in state elections throughout the 21st century. No Democratic Party candidate has won any statewide election, and Democrats have consistently been the MINORITY PARTY in state politics. Despite losses at the polls, Democratic Party candidates sometimes get a large minority of votes for statewide offices. In the 2016 presidential election, for example, Democratic candidate Hillary Clinton received 43.2% of the statewide vote for President, while Republican candidate Donald Trump received 52.2%.[386] Ross Ramsey of the *Texas Tribune* provided the following assessment of Texas voters during the 2016 election: "Tuesday's election results offer further evidence that Texas mirrors America, with urban voters strongly favoring Democrats, while rural and many suburban voters favor Republicans."[387] Trump was the favored presidential candidate in 227 Texas counties in 2016, winning a solid majority of rural Texas and multitudes of medium-sized cities. By contrast, Clinton won 27 counties, including some of the most populated ones such as Bexar, Dallas, El Paso, Fort Bend, Harris, Hidalgo, and Travis counties. Democratic candidates received a higher percentage of votes in large cities than in previous elections, and President Trump fared worse than any Republican running statewide in 2016.[388] None of the Republican candidates for state offices in 2016 received more than 56% of the vote.[389]

Conclusion

Those who value divided government and view an opposition party as an instrument to limit the will of an electoral majority will be discouraged by the study of Texas politics. The Democratic Party dominated Texas politics and government from 1872–1952, and the Republican Party has dominated state government since 1998.

Two-party competition occurred from 1952–1998 during the era of ticket-splitting. Texas's Republican voters do, however, have reasons to be optimistic about the current political divide in the state. Republican Party candidates consistently win at the polls, and Texas Republicans serving in the state legislature work to enact laws that are reflective of the party as a whole. But, as Erica Greider of *Texas Monthly* explains, there are potential drawbacks to the party's dominance in the state:

> [G]eneral elections are foregone conclusions, the only contests that matter are Republican primaries, and the path to victory lies in running as far right as possible. Under those conditions, a small subset of conservatives can hijack the political debate and many feel entitled to do so. That's how a once obscure issue like open carry became a top priority for the government of Texas and for the 27 million people it supposedly serves.[390]

Open carry had not yet passed when she wrote that article, and she thought most Texans would not be impacted by such a law.[391] Her criticisms in the above quote could be applied more broadly to institutions in Texas and give readers something to consider even if they are satisfied with the current state of Texas politics.

Key Terms

Secretary of State	election administrators
precinct chair	county chairs
county executive committee	state executive committee
state party chair	open primary system
closed primary system	straight party voting
ticket splitting	straight-ticket voting
political parties	interest groups
campaign finance committees	lobbying
political action committees (PACs)	issue advocacy
Grange	membership interest groups
non-member groups	government organizations
factions	third parties
Greenback Party	People's Party
party platform	grassroots efforts
Whig Party	Unionist Party
yellow dog Democrat	John G. Tower

Smith v. Allwright

24th Amendment

"Dirty Thirty"

Texas Constitutional Convention of 1974

William "Bill" Clements

Ann Richards

George W. Bush

unified government

Rick Perry

Texas Model

supermajority

campus carry

minority party

poll tax

Sharpstown Stock-Fraud Scandal

blue dog Democrats

Kay Bailey Hutchison

Tom Craddick

redistricting

Father's Day Massacre

abortion

House Bill 2

open carry

Unit 3: The Three Branches of Texas Government

Unit 2 discussed Texas politics in the context of the American federalism and the role of elections, political parties, and interest groups in the state. We turn our attention in Unit 3 to the three branches of Texas government created by the Texas Constitution of 1876. The chapters comprising Units 1 and 2 provide the foundations for understanding the current Texas Constitution and some of the unique features of Texas government. Historically, the Constitution was written in response to the state's experience with Reconstruction and the governorship of Edmund Davis, and a political culture that embraced and continues to embrace rugged individualism and a strong belief in limited government. Today, the legislative, executive, and judicial branches of Texas government retain the basic structures created for them by the Constitution of 1876, as well as additional features added through constitutional amendments and state statutes. The astute reader of Unit 3 will soon recognize how the state's interest in limited government is reflected in the numerous divisions of government power that are hallmarks of the Texas Constitution.

Chapter 6

The Texas Legislative Branch

Chapter 6 discusses the roles of the Texas legislature, state policy making, and legislative process in the Texas legislature. After reading this chapter students should understand:

▸ The leadership and roles of the Texas House of Representatives and Texas Senate
▸ The legislative processes of the Texas House and Texas Senate
▸ The interaction of the state legislature with other parts of state government
▸ The unique features of the Texas legislative branch of government

Introduction

The auxiliary precautions James Madison set forth in *Federalist* No. 51—separation of powers and federalism—can sometimes be confusing to observers of American government. Separation of powers divides power between the three branches of government (legislative, executive, and judicial), and federalism further divides power between the national government and state governments. Madison's auxiliary precautions are constitutional mechanisms intentionally designed to ensure that government power in the United States system is not concentrated in one person, branch, or level of government, and the inefficiency that results from dividing up government power serves to protect the political values of limited government and individual rights. Like the United States Constitution, the Texas Constitution of 1876 was written to limit government, as discussed in Chapter 3, and creates a system of government that embraces separation of powers and federalism. Separation of powers divides state power between three branches of state government—the legislative, executive, and judicial branches—and further divides power between the different levels of state government. DILLON'S RULE, as discussed in Chapter 4, holds that local governments (counties and cities) are creatures of the states. Local governments are permitted in Texas to enact legislation governing their respective spheres within the parameters allowed them through state law. Because of Dillon's Rule, legislative process in the United States does not stop with the United States Congress passing laws concerning the nation and the Texas Legislature passing laws concerning the state. Rather, the legislative process extends along the lines of federalism, from the nation to the state to the county commissioners' courts enacting laws concerning Texas counties, to city councils passing laws and ordinances concerning cities, and school boards and other special districts passing laws and ordinances that govern their special districts. Much of the legislative activity of state and local governments in the United States has focused on the "POLICE POWERS," or traditional government functions of the states, to regulate the safety, health, and morals of its citizens. This chapter focuses on the roles and processes of the state legislature and elaborates upon the ways in which the law making function of the Texas Legislature impacts the lives of Texans.

The Roles and Leadership of the Texas Legislature

The Texas Legislature is the primary law making body in the state. While the state executive branch is involved with enforcing law and the judicial branch with interpreting law, the legislature is busy performing its state constitutional duty of making laws. STATE STATUTES, or laws passed by the Texas Legislature, involve everything from wearing a helmet while riding a motorcycle to carrying concealed firearms, requiring childhood vaccinations for school-aged children, and appropriating money for state teachers, school districts, prisons, and roads. Like the United States Congress, the Texas Legislature is BICAMERAL and consists of the House of Representatives and Senate. Members are elected from state House and state Senate districts that roughly contain equal populations per chamber district. House districts are 1/150th of the state's population (meaning there are 150 members of the Texas House) and Senate districts represent roughly 1/31st of the state's population (meaning there are 31 members of the Texas Senate). Members of the Texas House are elected to two-year terms, and members of the Texas Senate are elected to four-year terms.

The Texas House and Texas Senate have different methods of selecting the leaders in their respective chambers. The Texas House is presided over by the SPEAKER OF THE HOUSE. The Speaker is selected by the members of the House and is therefore typically a member of the political party that holds a majority in the chamber. The Speaker is empowered to select the chairs and members of all House committees and subcommittees that perform the essential legislative functions of drafting, reviewing, revising, and enacting state laws. Unlike the United States Congress, not all committee chairs in either the Texas House or the Texas Senate are necessarily members of the majority party. The Speaker is free to select whomever he or she chooses to chair House committees and subcommittees, and a small number of chairs are normally members of the minority party. The PRESIDENT OF THE TEXAS SENATE also selects the members and chairs to serve on all Senate committees and subcommittees. But, unlike the Speaker of the House, the President of the Texas Senate is not chosen by the members of the chamber; rather, he or she is elected by the state's voters along with several other statewide officials in elections held in non-presidential even-numbered years. The President of the Texas Senate is the LIEUTENANT GOVERNOR, a position that is constitutionally part of the executive branch and therefore discussed in greater detail in Chapter 7.

The state House and Senate also differ in terms of their respective powers and constitutional obligations. The Senate is generally considered the more prestigious of the two chambers and is entrusted with responsibilities not delegated to the House. First, if a governor or other state official is considered for IMPEACHMENT from office, the House determines whether or not to impeach the official, but the Senate decides on whether the official should subsequently be removed from office. Only one Texas governor has been impeached and removed from office. James E. "Farmer Jim" Ferguson was convicted by the Texas Senate in 1917 on several charges including those stemming from a fight over control of the University of Texas.

For the Record: The Impeachment of Governor James E. "Farmer Jim" Ferguson and Subsequent Election of "Ma" Ferguson

Texas is home to the second female governor in United States history. The first woman governor, Nellie Ross, was elected Governor of Wyoming in 1925 in a special election to replace her late husband. Fifteen days later, MIRIAM "MA" FERGUSON was inaugurated as the Governor of Texas. Ferguson, like Ross, "replaced" her husband in the governor's mansion; however, it was not her husband's death that compelled "Ma" to run for office. Governor JAMES "FARMER JIM" FERGUSON was impeached by the Texas House of Representatives and removed from office by the Texas Senate after trying to remove public officials who opposed him (namely, members of the University of Texas board of regents) from office.

When the Texas Supreme Court blocked Farmer Jim's attempt to get his name on the gubernatorial ballot in 1924, his wife threw her hat into the ring. "Ma" quickly assured Texans that if elected she would follow the advice of her husband, and Texans would therefore be gaining "two governors for the price of one." Her campaign was based on four primary platforms: vindicating the Ferguson name, cutting state appropriations, condemning the Ku Klux Klan, and opposing the passage of new liquor laws.[392] "Ma" Ferguson easily defeated the Klan-supported prohibitionist candidate, Felix Robertson, in the Democratic gubernatorial primary, then handily defeated the Republican nominee, George C. Butte, a former dean of the University of Texas School of Law, in the general election.

Controversies including increases in state appropriations, irregularities in pardons and paroles, and supposed kickbacks for state highway construction contracts surrounded her first term in office. She was defeated by Attorney General Daniel James Moody in the 1926 gubernatorial election and again in 1930 by Ross Sterling.[393] The electoral defeats did not thwart "Ma's" desire to serve as Texas Governor. She again ran and was again elected to governor in 1932, and after a brief retirement from public life, was defeated in the 1940 governor's race by radio announcer W. Lee "Pappy" O'Daniel (inducted into the Texas Radio Hall of Fame in 2015 for his contributions to Texas music including promotion of the Texas band the Light Crust

Doughboys and its members Bob Wills and Milton Brown).[394]

Second, the Texas House does not have a formal say in whether or not an official appointed by the governor receives confirmation. Unlike the President of the United States, the Texas Governor has very limited appointment powers and most high-ranking state executive officials are elected. Some important chairs and members of state boards and commissions are, however, appointed by the governor but must be approved by a 2/3 vote of the Texas Senate in order to assume office. An example of a governor-appointed, Senate-confirmed state board is the Texas Board of Pardons and Paroles. Many people assume the act of pardoning a state offense is strictly at the governor's discretion when, in fact, a pardon must first be approved by the Board of Pardons and Paroles. Other examples of governor-appointed and Senate-confirmed board memberships include those to the Texas State University Board of Regents, which oversees Lamar University, Sam Houston State University, and other colleges and universities in the Texas State system, and the Texas Alcoholic Beverage Commission (TABC), which regulates all phases of the alcoholic beverage industry in Texas. Unlike the vast authority held by the President of the United States to remove appointed officials from office (discussed in Chapter 7), the removal powers of the Texas Governor are greatly restricted by state constitutional and statutory requirements.

The Texas Legislature and Policymaking

The Texas Constitution requires a PART-TIME LEGISLATURE, meaning the state legislature only meets in REGULAR SESSION once every other year, in odd-numbered years, for a period not to exceed 140 days. Regular sessions begin in January and end in late spring—a period of time that is very brief given the legislature must address in regular session its entire agenda including the state budget (which must last two years because of constitutional limits on regular legislative sessions); individual budget items such as appropriations to social services, state teachers, colleges and universities, and state prisons; and, proposed non-appropriation bills such as campus weapons carry, restroom accommodations based on gender identity or biological sex at birth, and sanctuary cities. If the legislature does not adopt a budget or address a bill the governor considers important during its regular session, the governor may call a SPECIAL LEGISLATIVE SESSION. Special legislative sessions may only be called by the governor, require members of the legislature to return to Austin to consider unresolved legislative matters, and may last no more than 30 days. Although the governor has the power to call and set the agenda for a special session, he or she is not given the authority to force a vote by the legislature. The governor may call a special session specifically for the purpose of gaining legislation he or she desires, such as a finalized budget or the passage of a specific bill; however, the session may produce an opposite result by the legislature refusing to pass the governor's proposals. If the governor's proposals are not passed in special session, the governor may call another special session. There are no constitutional or statutory limits on the number of special sessions a governor can call; however, informal constraints do exist given the financial costs incurred by Texas taxpayers for special sessions is extremely high, and the professional and personal lives of lives of legislators are disrupted by having to return to Austin to consider matters unresolved in the regular session or a previous special session.

Service in the Texas legislature is designed to be a NON-PROFESSIONAL, part-time position. Members of the Texas Legislature, including the Speaker of the House, currently earn less than $8,000 per year for their legislative service. Extremely low pay requires state legislators to have jobs or income derived from sources outside of their legislative service, and members with extra-legislative careers must by necessity have jobs that allow them to take off work in order to perform their legislative duties. Since the average Texan does not have a job that allows him or her to be absent from work for a minimum of 140 days every other year and take off additional time to attend special sessions and handle legislative matters and maintain constituency contacts outside the regular session, membership in the Texas legislature is overwhelmingly comprised of individuals with greater personal wealth and resources than those held by the average Texan and is not reflective of the overall racial, ethnic, and gender demographics of Texas. Nearly 2/3 of state lawmakers were non-Hispanic white Texans in 2017, while that demographic label describes only 43% of the state's population. Also, men were close to 80% of lawmakers that year.[395]

The Legislative Process in Texas

The legislative process in Texas actually begins before a bill enters the state House or Senate. A legislator, interest group, or private individual must first have an idea about a new state law or the need to repeal an existing law. Interest groups and private citizens must find a state representative or senator willing to support the bill and introduce it in the legislature. Figure 6.1 demonstrates the legislative processes in the Texas House and Texas Senate and provides readers valuable information about how an individual might be able to impact state law through representative democracy and the legislative process.

Legislative processes in the House and Senate differ slightly, but their commonalities shed light on how bills become state law. First, a bill may originate in either legislative chamber. The chambers each perform three READINGS of the bill before it can be considered for passage into law. The first reading occurs when a bill is introduced. Only the bill's caption is read and, based on the caption, is referred by the Speaker of the House or the President of the Senate to an appropriate committee in their respective chamber.[396] There is no vote in the full chamber immediately following the first reading of a bill. Second, after a bill enters committee, all committee business on the bill must be conducted in open meetings and no official action or vote may be taken except in a meeting that is open to the public.[397] The committee to which the bill is assigned decides how to address the bill. It may vote to reject the bill, which in political terms means the bill is dead and ceases to be considered for passage; leave the bill pending or refuse to give it a hearing, which also essentially "kills" the bill; or approve the bill without any amendments. The committee may also vote to amend the bill and approve it in its amended version.

Legislative process in the Texas House of Representatives begins with the drafting of the bill. After the House committee approves the bill, it moves on to the PRINTING AND DISTRIBUTION stage. The committee report is printed and distributed to members of the House and sent to a House calendar committee to determine when the bill will be considered by the House floor (the entire chamber). Once set on the calendar, the bill proceeds to a SECOND READING where the bill is read aloud to the House and open to debate and discussion by members of the chamber. Amendments proposed after the second reading must be approved by over half of the members present in order for the amendments to be added to the bill.[398] The bill proceeds to a THIRD READING after it is approved by a majority of the chamber's membership and is again subject to debate and amendments. Amendments proposed to a bill after the third reading require a 2/3rd rather than simple majority vote of the House in order to be included as part of the bill.[399] If the House votes against the bill after either the second or third reading, the bill is "killed." But, if the House approves the bill it becomes ENGROSSED, meaning any approved and applicable amendments are added to the original bill before it is sent to the Texas Senate. Regardless of whether a bill originates in the House or Senate, once it is approved by the original chamber, it must proceed to the other chamber for passage before going to the governor for approval or veto.

The original stages of the legislative process in the Texas Senate are almost identical to those in the House of Representatives. After the first reading of a bill, the Lieutenant Governor (acting as President of the Senate) refers the bill to committee. The Senate committee then faces the same set of choices faced by a House committee: it may vote to reject the bill; leave the bill pending or refuse to give it a hearing; approve the bill without any amendments; or amend the bill and approve it in its amended version. Once approved, the bill enters the printing and distribution stage and is scheduled in the Senate's regular order of business. The Texas Senate may then consider the bill; but, unlike Texas House rules, Senate rules require not only that the bill be placed on the chamber's calendar but also that a vote to suspend the regular order of business occur before the full Senate can consider a bill. The Texas House does not have a similar SUSPENSION OF ORDER RULE. Suspending the regular order of business of the Senate requires a 3/5th vote of the chamber and stems from a Texas Senate tradition of placing bills with little or no chance of passage or highly controversial bills with only limited support at the top of the legislative agenda at the beginning of the session. The Senate cannot move forward to consider other, more viable legislation unless and until a 3/5th vote is gained to suspend the regular order of business to allow the chamber to consider less viable bills. If a suspension of business order is not secured, the bills at the top of the agenda will not progress further for consideration by the chamber. If a 3/5th vote is obtained, the bill moves on to a second reading and debate and discussion by the chamber's members.

Amendments at this stage of the legislative process of the Senate require the support of only a simple majority of present and voting Senate members.[400] If amendments are approved, the bill goes on to a third reading. After the third reading, any proposed amendments to the bill must receive a 2/3rd vote of the chamber in order to be added to a bill.[401] Bills that fail to gain a majority vote of the Senate after the third reading are "killed," and bills that receive a majority vote pass the chamber and proceed to the next step in the legislative process.

Once approved by the chamber in which it originates, a bill must then proceed to the other chamber for passage before going to the governor for approval or veto. Let's assume a bill passes the Texas House and moves to the Senate for consideration. During Senate debate and voting on the bill, the Senate votes to approve amendments to the original bill. Since the addition of Senate amendments changes the contents of the original bill approved by the House, the bill with the newly added Senate amendments will be printed and distributed to members of the House. The House will then vote on whether or not to concur with the Senate amendments. If the House concurs with the amendments, the House Clerk will enroll the bill, both the Speaker of the House and the Lieutenant Governor will sign it, and the bill will move forward to the Governor's desk. If the House votes to refuse concurrence of the Senate amendments, a CONFERENCE COMMITTEE consisting of five members from each chamber will convene to discuss and draft a report that is subsequently printed and distributed to the members of both chambers. The report is then voted on by the members of both chambers. If either chamber rejects the report, the bill dies. If the report is approved by both chambers, the House Clerk will enroll the bill, the Speaker and Lieutenant Governor will sign it, and the bill will proceed to Governor.

Figure 6.1

Process for House Bills
Texas Legislature

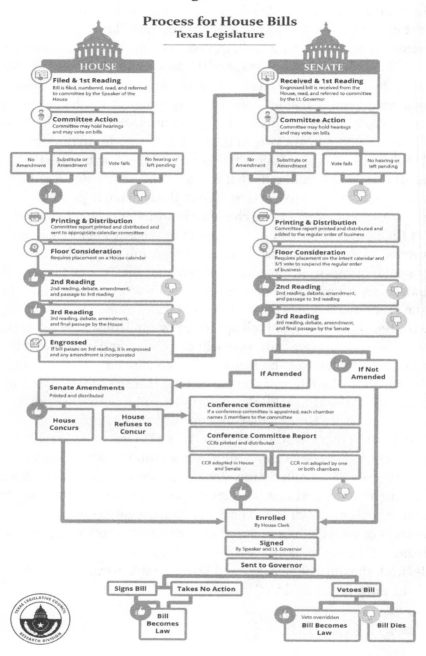

Source: "Process for House Bills: Texas Legislature." *Texas Legislative Council: Research Division*, www.tlc.state.tx.us/docs/billprocess/BillProcessHouse_Final.pdf. Accessed 17 Nov. 2017

There is no guarantee a bill approved by both chambers of the legislature will be enacted into law. The Governor has ten days from the date of the passage of the bill to act on it. He or she may sign the bill, take no action on the bill, or VETO the bill. If the Governor signs the bill, it becomes law with the Governor's signature. If he or she takes no action on the bill within ten days, the bill becomes law without the Governor's signature on the eleventh day. If the Governor vetoes the bill, the bill is returned to the chamber in which it originated for a vote on an override. A 2/3rd majority of both chambers of the legislature are required to override a gubernatorial veto.[402] A 2/3rd majority vote of both chambers is extremely difficult to achieve, and the vast majority of vetoes by the Texas Governor, like those by the President of the United States, fail to be overridden.

Conclusion

Legislative process in the two chambers that comprise the Texas legislative branch are similar with the exception of unique traditions, such as the suspension of order rule in the Texas Senate. The roles of the Speaker of the House and the Lieutenant Governor are also similar in terms of legislative process. We will discover in the next chapter that the Lieutenant Governor holds constitutional and statutory authority in both legislative and executive branches of government and is widely considered to be the most powerful statewide official in Texas.

Key Terms

Dillon's Rule	police powers
state statutes	bicameralism
Speaker of the House	President of the Senate
impeachment	"Ma" Ferguson
James Ferguson	part-time legislature
regular sessions	special sessions
non-professional legislature	readings
printing and distribution	second reading
third reading	engrossed
suspension of order rule	conference committees
veto power	

Chapter 7

The Texas Executive Branch

The Texas executive branch bears little resemblance to the United States executive branch. The notion that the Texas governor serves as the state equivalent to the president at the national level is false, and must be discarded before delving into a study of the Texas executive branch. This section describes the Texas plural executive and discusses the ways in which the state executive branch differs from the national executive branch. At the conclusion of this subsection, students should be able to identify:

- The unique features of the Texas executive branch and the ways it differs from the national executive branch
- The key offices of the Texas plural executive and the roles and functions of each office
- The ways in which separate elections of members of the executive branch impacts Texas government
- The role of state boards and commissions in the Texas executive branch

Differences between the National Executive and the Texas Executive

Readers of this textbook have likely gained familiarity with the executive branch of the United States. A summary of some of the features of the national executive branch serves to highlight the numerous ways in which the Texas executive branch differs from the United States executive branch. First, the national executive branch has one clear leader—the President of the United States. The president's immense power over the executive branch is the result of both historical change and constitutional mandates. Although the United States Constitution states that the president and vice president are to be chosen separately, the common practice of selecting vice presidents since the 19th century has been for electors to the Electoral College to pledge to vote for the presidential and vice presidential candidates that are together presented by a given political party. The modern practice of selecting presidents and vice presidents together has served to eliminate problems that surfaced early in the nation's history when electoral procedure, established before the rise of modern American political parties, called for the candidate with the highest number of votes to serve as president, and the candidate with the second highest number of votes to serve as vice president. Today, the practice of electors pledging to vote for the winning party's presidential/vice presidential ticket largely eliminates the likelihood that a president and vice president from competing political parties will serve together in office. Furthermore, presidents are constitutionally empowered to hand select the top executive officials that will serve under him or her during the duration of their term, subject to confirmation by the Senate. Appointed executive officials act as the heads of national administrative agencies charged with assisting the president in carrying out the executive duties and functions of the nation. High-ranking executive officials serve completely at the discretion of the president. While Senate approval is required before a federal executive appointee may assume office, it is not required when a president decides to remove an appointed official from office. James Comey, Jr.'s appointment to the high-ranking executive post of Director of the Federal Bureau of Investigations, for example, required Senate confirmation when he was first appointed to the position by President Barack Obama in 2013; however, President Donald Trump's decision to remove Comey from the office in 2017 was unilateral and required no Senate approval.

In addition to the president's authority and discretion over personnel that comprise the top tier of the national executive branch, three features of the national executive should be noted before beginning our discussion of the Texas executive. The first involves the 22ND AMENDMENT to the United States Constitution. The 22nd Amendment, ratified in 1951, establishes presidential term limits. No United States president may be elected to more than two consecutive terms. Second, in CLINTON V. CITY OF NEW YORK (1998),[403] the United

States Supreme Court ruled that presidential LINE ITEM VETOES violated the Presentment Clause of the United States Constitution. Line item veto allows executives to reject or eliminate one part of a budget bill while leaving the remainder of the bill intact. After the *Clinton* decision, presidents retain the power of regular veto (the ability to reject an entire bill subject to override by a two-thirds majority vote by both chambers of Congress), but no longer have the power to line item veto part of a budget bill presented to him or her by the legislative branch. Finally, presidents have the power to appoint judges to the federal judiciary. Federal judges, upon nomination by the President and confirmation by the Senate, serve life terms on the bench except in cases of resignation, retirement, and impeachment.

The Offices Comprising the Texas Plural Executive

Executive authority and discretion over personnel, term limits, the president's inability to line item veto, and the president's power to appoint judges are four major ways in which the Texas executive branch differs from the national executive branch. Many students of Texas government are surprised to learn that executive power in the state is divided between a number of state executive offices, and that in the division of power the governor holds the least amount of constitutional power. While national executive power is concentrated in one leader—the president—state executive power in Texas is constitutionally divided between six elected officials and one appointed official together known as the PLURAL EXECUTIVE. The elected members of the plural executive are the Governor, Lieutenant Governor, Comptroller of Public Accounts, Land Commissioner, Agriculture Commissioner, and Attorney General. The seventh member, the Secretary of State, is appointed by the governor.

The elected members of the Texas plural executive are selected by the state's voters separately, meaning voters are free to select candidates from different parties to different executive offices. Unlike the United States system in which the president and vice president are for all practical purposes chosen together on the same ticket and the president is able to hand-pick all high-ranking executive officials subject to confirmation by the Senate, the Texas system allows the state's voters to choose the members of the plural executive from across

135

parties and to "split their tickets" between parties and offices. Examples of ticket splitting by Texas voters were evident in the election of 1990 when Democrat Ann Richards was elected to serve as Governor and Republican Rick Perry was elected to serve as Agricultural Commissioner, and in the election of 1994 when Republican George W. Bush was elected to serve as Governor and Democrat Bob Bullock was elected to serve as Lieutenant Governor. The ability to ticket split means the Texas plural executive may at any time consist of members from different parties with different ideological views on the role of state government and on how the Texas executive branch should function.

Ticket splitting by Texas voters significantly declined in the late 20th century. Since 2000, every elected member of the Texas plural executive has been a member of the Republican Party. One-party dominance of the Texas executive branch does not, however, necessarily mean cohesion within the plural executive. Separate elections promotes a political climate in which members of the same party are not directly dependent on one another for reelection and therefore tend to appeal directly to the state's voters rather than to the party or fellow office seekers and office holders. A governor or other member of the plural executive may, for example, be deeply concerned with organizational efficiency and want all members of the plural executive to work well together. But, other executive officials may determine they are better able to fulfill the duties and obligations of their office by working independent of the other members of the plural executive and have a greater chance at reelection if they promote themselves, their agendas, and their professional successes among the voters rather than directly among their elected colleagues. Independence and self-promotion are particularly important for officials hoping to use their current executive positions as a launching pad from which to gain electoral support for possible future runs for more visible (if less powerful) executive offices, such as governor.

Lack of cohesion in the Texas plural executive is further exacerbated by the fact that the framers of the Texas Constitution clearly intended state executive power to be divided among several offices rather than concentrated in the hands of one person or group of people. The Texas Constitution grants the GOVERNOR very limited powers, and the powers that are retained in the office overwhelmingly emanate from statutory grants of power by the Texas legislature and informal political skills such as persuasion, charm, and charisma that may be possessed by the person holding the office. The governor has statutory or constitutional authority to appoint the secretary of state and fill offices left vacant due to death, retirement, or impeachment until an election can be held; to veto legislation passed by the state legislature subject to a two-thirds majority override vote by both chambers of the legislature; and to call out the Texas National Guard when the Guard has not been federalized (called into service) by the President of the United States. Unlike the president, the Texas governor also has the power of line item veto over budget bills. If, for example, the governor wanted to approve all sections of a budget bill except for one that appropriates funds to construct a new building at Texas A&M University, the governor could use the power of line item veto to reject only that section of the bill that appropriates building funds for Texas A&M while leaving intact all other sections of the bill. A standard (non-line item) veto by the governor eliminates a bill in its entirety and is subject to a two-thirds majority vote in both legislative chambers.

Also, unlike the national executive branch, the governor as well as all elected members of the Texas plural executive are not subject to term limits. State-level elected executives may continue to be reelected as long as the voters of Texas continue to choose them over their opponents. Former Texas Governor Rick Perry, for example, began his tenure as governor in December 2000 when, as Lieutenant Governor, he assumed the office of Governor of Texas after Governor George W. Bush vacated the office to become President of the United States. Perry was subsequently elected governor in the 2002 elections and reelected in the 2006 and 2010 elections. Despite the lack of term limits and the power of line item veto, the governor has extremely limited discretionary authority over the personnel in the state's executive branch. All decisions by the governor to dismiss executive branch personnel must be approved by the Texas Senate, unlike the sweeping power of the President of the United States to remove high-ranking executive officials without approval by the United States Senate.

The governor may also remove state judges under particular circumstances. District court judges, as well as judges serving on the intermediate courts of appeals, the Texas Supreme Court, and the Court of Criminal Appeals, may be dismissed by the governor "on the address of two-thirds of each House of the Legislature, for willful neglect of duty, incompetency, habitual drunkenness, oppression in office, or other reasonable cause which shall not be sufficient ground for impeachment ..." (Texas Constitution, Article 15, Section 8). The accused judge must be notified of the alleged cause(s) for removal and is entitled to a hearing to defend himself or herself before the legislature votes on this matter.[404] The authority that the Texas Constitution allows the governor to remove state judges under limited circumstances is consistent with the overall design of the Texas state government in that the governor's authority is far from absolute and is subject to legislative approval.

The office of the LIEUTENANT GOVERNOR—not the governor—possesses the greatest amount of constitutional and statutory power in the Texas plural executive. The Texas Constitution establishes the office of lieutenant governor as part of the state executive branch, but in order to keep the officeholder in check, the powers designated to the office are largely legislative rather than executive in nature. Two legislative powers held by the lieutenant governor deserve elaboration. First, state statutes empower the lieutenant governor to serve as the chair of the very powerful LEGISLATIVE BUDGET BOARD (LBB). The LBB is responsible for preparing the state's legislative budget, which is subsequently submitted to the state House and Senate for approval. Second, the Texas Constitution calls for the lieutenant governor to serve as President of the Texas Senate. You will recall in our studies of American government that the vice-president of the United States serves as president of the Senate; however, the legislative powers granted to the United States President of the Senate are extremely limited and consist almost exclusively of casting the tie-breaking vote in case of a tie vote in the Senate. The Texas lieutenant governor also has the power to break a tie vote; but, his or her role as President of the Texas Senate is much more expansive than that of the President of the United States Senate. As President of the Texas Senate, the lieutenant governor presides over the Senate in ways similar to those of the Speaker of the House presiding over the House of Representatives. The lieutenant governor has immense influence over the Texas legislature in his or her ability to select the chairs and members of all Senate committees and subcommittees.

For the Record: The Plural Executive and the Rise to Governor

The longest serving Texas lieutenant governor to-date is WILLIAM "BILL" P. HOBBY, JR. The son of Texas governor William P. Hobby, Sr. and United States Cabinet Secretary Oveta Culp Hobby, he served as Lieutenant Governor for eighteen years (1973 to 1991). Hobby was succeeded in the office by BOB BULLOCK, a colorful political personality described by Rick Lyman of the *New York Times* as "among the last of the earthy, string-pulling, hard-living political giants who used to sprout in Texas as thick as bluebonnets." Before becoming Lieutenant Governor, Bullock served sixteen years as state comptroller.

Texas Agriculture Commissioner RICK PERRY succeeded Bullock as Lieutenant Governor in 1998. Two state constitutional amendments proved to be of particular political benefit to Perry. First, an amendment to Section 4 of the Texas Constitution, ratified in 1972, increased the term of the office of the Texas governor from two to four years.[405] George W. Bush was the first Texas governor to be elected to two consecutive four-year terms;[406] however, he vacated the office in the middle of his second term to become President of the United States. When the governor's office was vacated by President Bush, Lieutenant Governor Perry, elected to the office only one year before, assumed the governorship due to a state constitutional amendment ratified in 1999 providing that the lieutenant governor succeed to the office of governor when the governor-elect is unable to serve.[407] (A previous state constitutional amendment ratified in 1948 held that the lieutenant governor would assume the governorship only in cases of a governor-elect's death, disability, or failure to qualify.)[408] Perry was elected to his first full term as governor in 2002.

Neither the Texas Constitution nor any state statute has mandated term limits for Texas elected officials. Members of the plural executive and the legislature may serve for as long as the voters continue to elect them to office. Governor Perry was elected to three consecutive four-year terms and served as governor from 2000 to 2015. He ran two unsuccessful campaigns for the United States presidency (2012 and 2016), and in 2016 was named Secretary of Energy by President Donald Trump.

The COMPTROLLER OF PUBLIC ACCOUNTS also plays a critical role in the functioning of the state. The comptroller sets the state legislature's spending limit for the BIENNIUM, or two-year legislative cycle. Unlike the United States Congress, the Texas legislature meets in regular session only once every other year in odd-numbered years; therefore, the budget set by the state comptroller must project and apply to a two-year rather than one-year legislative cycle. The comptroller's budgeted spending limit is important because it helps ensure the legislature does not spend more money than the state can afford. Unlike the United States Congress, the Texas legislature is constitutionally restricted by a BALANCED BUDGET requirement, meaning the legislature cannot enact appropriation bills without the existence or projected existence of state funds available to cover the cost of the appropriation.

The three remaining elected offices in the Texas plural executive have less direct involvement with the legislature than do the governor, lieutenant governor, and comptroller, and they primarily work to carry out and enforce state policies and administrative regulations. The LAND COMMISSIONER, elected by the voters of Texas to four-year terms, manages all state-owned lands, mineral rights, assets, and income derived from Texas public lands. Managing Texas lands and their assets is no small task given that Texas holds land and mineral rights totaling nearly 13 million acres.[409] Texas lands include vast properties in West Texas; the Gulf Coast region including beaches, bays, and all "submerged" lands 10.35 miles out into the Gulf of Mexico; and acreage and timberlands in East Texas.[410] The primary responsibility of the GENERAL LAND OFFICE is to lease public lands for the benefit of the Permanent School Fund, an endowment fund established in 1876 specifically designated to benefit Texas public education.[411] The office also manages royalties derived from oil and gas production on state lands; is responsible for developing state environmental protection policies; and administers services for Texas veterans through public land income. The AGRICULTURE COMMISSIONER, also elected to four-year terms, is responsible for regulating all fuel pumps, weights and measures, residential and commercial pesticide use and application, and organic agricultural products. The agriculture commissioner's office is also charged with protecting and advocating on behalf of the state's $106 billion agricultural sector, which comprises 10% of the

Texas economy;[412] overseeing healthy living initiatives such as national school lunch and breakfast programs; providing financial assistance to Texas farmers and ranchers; and offering infrastructure grants to rural communities.[413] Occasionally, the agriculture commissioner is faced with politically charged issues such as recent approval by the Texas Department of Agriculture (headed by the agriculture commissioner) for private individuals and the state to use the poison warfarin to help control the state's estimated 2 million wild hogs.[414] The state ATTORNEY GENERAL, also elected by Texas voters to four-year terms, serves as legal counsel for the state. The Texas Constitution charges the attorney general with defending the laws and Constitution of Texas; representing the state in federal and state litigation; and approving public bond issues. Over time, nearly 2000 state statutes have greatly expanded the responsibilities of the office to include representation of the state's interests in cases involving health, safety, and consumer regulations; educational outreach programs; and protection of the elderly and disabled. The attorney general is also statutorily charged with collecting court-ordered child support and administering the state's Crime Victims' Compensation Fund.[415]

The only non-elected member of the Texas plural executive is the SECRETARY OF STATE. The Texas secretary of state is appointed by the governor, confirmed by the state Senate, and is constitutionally charged with overseeing all elections in the state. While elections and voter registration are carried out by Texas county officials, the secretary of state is responsible for maintaining over 14 million voter registration records on behalf of the state as well as administering and enforcing the Texas Election Code that regulates Texas voters, elections, voting systems, candidates, and political parties.[416] Additionally, the Business and Public Filings Division of the Office of Secretary of State maintains filings and records related to Texas corporations and public organizations, and publishes the weekly *Texas Register*, which publicizes official state rules, meetings, opinions, and proclamations.[417] The responsibilities and functions of the Texas secretary of state have historically held no resemblance to the United States secretary of state in terms of the latter's role as senior official to the president in matters concerning foreign policy. More recently, however, the role of the Texas secretary of state has been extended into the realm of foreign policy through executive orders issued by the Governor of Texas. Today, the appointed secretary of state serves as the governor's lead liaison for Texas Border and Mexican Affairs and chief international protocol officer of the state. As chief international protocol officer, the secretary of state receives international dignitaries and delegations on behalf of the governor and represents the governor at meetings and events attended by the international diplomatic corps.[418]

Texas Executive Branch Boards and Commissions

In addition to major agencies that are part of the plural executive, Texas has approximately 200 state boards and commissions that constitute a large portion of the state's executive branch but are not officially considered part of the plural executive.[419] The roles and responsibilities of state boards and commissions are to carry out and enforce laws passed by the Texas legislature and to establish and promulgate rules and policies that govern their respective administrative agencies. Among the most important state boards, commissions, and agencies are the State Board of Education, the Texas Board of Criminal Justice, and the Texas Alcoholic Beverage Commission. The STATE BOARD OF EDUCATION (SBOE) sets policies and standards for Texas schools including curricular requirements, textbooks, graduation requirements, and final review of rules governing the State Board for Educator Certification.[420] The SBOE also serves as the policymaking body of the Texas Education Agency, which coordinates all primary and secondary public school activity. Members of the State Board of Education are elected by the voters of the state from single-member districts to serve four-year terms. One commissioner of education is nominated by the elected board and appointed by the governor with the advice and consent of the Texas Senate.[421] The TEXAS BOARD OF CRIMINAL JUSTICE consists of nine members appointed by the governor to staggered six-year terms. The board is charged with overseeing Texas Department of Criminal Justice, which provides confinement, supervision, rehabilitation, and reintegration of the state's convicted felons,[422] and houses a number of state agencies including the Texas Board of Pardons and Paroles and the Office of the Inspector General. The TEXAS ALCOHOLIC BEVERAGE COMMISSION (TABC) regulates all phases of the alcoholic beverage industry in Texas. It consists of a three-member governing board appointed by the governor with the advice and consent of the Senate to staggered six-year terms. The Commission's duties include the regulation of sales, importation, manufacturing, transporting, and advertising of alcoholic beverages, as well as the collection of state taxes and fees on alcohol, which annually contribute to the state's coffers more than $300 million.[423]

Conclusion

Our review of the Texas executive branch highlights several unique features of the executive branch of government and demonstrates ways in which the Texas executive branch differs from the national executive branch. Members of the plural executive as well as those serving on various boards and commissions play important roles in the day-to-day operation of Texas government. While some high-ranking executive officials in Texas such as the secretary of state and members of the Board of Criminal Justice and the Alcoholic Beverage Commission are appointed by the governor with approval of the Senate, the governor may not remove appointed executive officials without the approval of the state Senate, and many important executive positions are elected directly by the voters of the state. The question of whether or not it is wise to vest Texas voters with such tremendous authority over the state's executive branch is a valid one particularly given the state's history of extremely low voter turnout in statewide elections. It is, however, clear that a majority of the framers of the Texas Constitution overwhelmingly preferred popular elections over gubernatorial appointments, especially in light of the post-Reconstruction, post-Edmund Davis era in which the current Constitution was written. As we will see in the following chapter on the Texas judicial branch, the framers' affinity for elections over appointments extended well beyond the selection of executive officials.

Key Terms

22nd Amendment	*Clinton v. City of New York*
line item veto	plural executive
Texas Governor	Lieutenant Governor
Legislative Budget Board	William "Bill" P. Hobby, Jr.

Bob Bullock

Rick Perry

Comptroller of Public Accounts

biennium

balanced budget

Land Commission

General Land Office

Agriculture Commissioner

Attorney General

Secretary of State

State Board of Education

Texas Board of Criminal Justice

Texas Alcoholic Beverage Commission

Chapter 8

The Texas Judiciary

Chapter 8 concludes Unit 3 and the review of the three branches of Texas government. It discusses the structure of the Texas judiciary and the ways in which the Texas judicial branch differs from the national judiciary. At the conclusion of the chapter, students should be able to identify:

▸ The unique features of the Texas judicial branch and the ways in which the state judiciary differs from the national judiciary
▸ Legal concepts relevant to understanding the structure and powers of Texas state courts
▸ The levels of courts that comprise the Texas judiciary and the roles and functions each level plays in the overall functioning of the state judiciary
▸ The ways in which the selection of judges in Texas differs from the selection of federal judges

Introduction

The third and most complicated branch of Texas government is the judicial branch. While the state and national judiciaries share some common features, they largely stand in sharp contrast to one another, especially in terms of their respective high court structures and methods of judicial selection. A brief summary of some of the relevant and important features of the federal judiciary will assist students in understanding the unique features of the Texas judiciary and the ways in which it differs from the national judiciary.

First, the United States judicial branch consists of one high court (the United States Supreme Court) that serves as the court of last and final resort on all matters of law in the country and is comprised of eight associate justices and one chief justice; twelve intermediate courts (the United States Courts of Appeals); and ninety-one lower federal courts (the United States District Courts).[424] Second, with the exception of magistrates, all federal judges are nominated by the president, confirmed by the Senate, and hold lifetime tenure except in cases of death, retirement, resignation, or impeachment. Third, JURISDICTION— the ability of a court to hear a particular type of case—is important to understanding the operations of both the federal judiciary and the state judiciary. Courts with ORIGINAL JURISDICTION such as federal district courts hear issues of fact and may empanel a jury of ordinary citizens to hear and decide the outcome of cases. Courts with APPELLATE JURISDICTION such as the Court of Appeals hear issues of law with judges sitting *EN BANC* (all together) or in panels of three in review of cases that come before them on appeal from the lower courts. The United States Supreme Court has both original and appellate jurisdiction with its original jurisdiction controlled by the United States Constitution and its appellate jurisdiction controlled by Congress. Another type of jurisdiction concerns the subject matter or types of cases a court is empowered to hear. Courts with CRIMINAL LAW jurisdiction hear cases involving violations of one or more state or federal laws designed to prevent one or more persons from causing victimized harm to another (i.e., murder, rape, theft, and assault). Courts with CIVIL LAW jurisdiction hear matters involving disputes between private individuals over non-criminal matters such as child custody and divorce, estate and will probates, personal injuries, and breaches of contract. Generally, federal courts have both criminal law and civil law jurisdiction.

The Texas judicial branch also consists of a high court system, intermediate appellate courts, and lower district courts. Original and appellate jurisdiction is designated to state courts in a way similar to that in the federal court, with high courts and intermediate courts generally having appellate jurisdiction and lower state district courts having original jurisdiction. Some Texas courts such as justice courts, county courts, and intermediate appellate courts hold both criminal law and civil law jurisdiction; however, particularly in densely populated areas, state district courts tend to hold specialized jurisdiction over one area of law such as criminal law, civil law, family law, or juvenile

146

justice. Finally, Texas is divided into geographical areas that contain appellate courts and district courts just as the United States is divided into geographical areas containing federal appellate courts and federal district court. As of March 2017, Texas had 14 state courts of appeals (as compared to 12 federal courts of appeals circuits) and 467 state district courts (as compared to 91 federal district courts). Beyond the existence of geographically divided lower court systems containing courts with original and appellate jurisdiction, the similarities between the structure of the United States judiciary and the Texas judiciary largely come to a close.

The Texas Bifurcated High Court System and State Appellate Process

The astute reader of the preceding section will have noticed that the term "high court system" rather than "Supreme Court" was used to describe the Texas judiciary—and for very good reason. Texas and Oklahoma are the only two states in the nation that have a BIFURCATED HIGH COURT system. A bifurcated high court system divides judicial power between two high courts with one court having civil law jurisdiction and the other court having criminal law jurisdiction. In Texas, the bifurcated high court system consists of one state Supreme Court and one state Court of Criminal Appeals (not to be confused with the state courts of appeals, to be discussed later in this chapter). The TEXAS SUPREME COURT is the highest court in the state over civil matters, and the TEXAS COURT OF CRIMINAL APPEALS is the highest court in the state over criminal matters. Both courts have appellate jurisdiction, and in their respective spheres (civil law and criminal law) are the highest courts of last resort in the state. The types of cases each court is empowered to hear are strictly defined by state constitutional and statutory law.

The concept of jurisdiction as it relates to the Texas judiciary is best explained in terms of a hypothetical state case. Let's assume, for example, a person enters into a contract with another individual to paint the interior and exterior of her business. The contract explicitly states "interior and exterior painting of commercial property" but contains neither a breakdown of services nor any reference to labor and supplies. The painter enters into the contract in good faith that the contracted amount is for labor only, and the business owner enters into the contract in good faith the amount includes both labor and supplies. Upon completion of the work, the painter hands the business owner a bill reflecting a charge of $80,000—an amount $20,000 over the amount set forth in the contract. Needless to say, words ensue between the business owner and the painter. (The fact that a discussion clarifying the terms of the contract should have been held *before* the parties agreed to the contract is irrelevant.) The business owner sues the painter for breach of contract and, after a long pre-trial period, the case is presented to a jury that ultimately delivers a judgment in favor of the business owner. But, during the trial the painter's attorney submitted into evidence a Texas statute that could be used to assist individuals and jurors in interpreting ambiguous contracts. The business owner's attorney in turn moved to strike the statute from the trial and the judge granted the attorney's request—meaning, the statute could not be presented to the jury for consideration during trial. The painter may not appeal the jury's final judgment simply because he lost the case or believes the jurors did not understand the facts of the case. Rather, his appeal must be based on an issue of law such as the trial court judge's decision to not allow the jury to consider the statute based on her interpretation of the Texas Code of Civil Procedure.

At this point in our hypothetical case the reader can easily surmise that issues of law are highly technical and require a great deal of legal training and expertise. For this reason, judges—not juries consisting of ordinary people—determine the outcome of appellate court cases. Assuming our case reaches the highest court in the state over civil matters—the Texas Supreme Court—the justices serving on the Court would consider relevant rules of civil procedure and evidence; the wording of the statute in question; the trial court judge's reasoning behind granting the request to strike evidence; and other matters of law relevant to the case before them. Should the Court determine the trial court judge's decision was consistent with the letter and spirit of state law and rules of civil procedure, the jury's decision at the trial court level would stand and the business owner would prevail. But, if the Court determined the judge's decision was not consistent with state rules and procedure, the case would be remanded back to the lower courts for a new trial that would include jury consideration of the evidence omitted in the original trial. While state and federal rules of

148

criminal procedure differ in important and substantial ways from those of civil procedure, the basic concept of appeals outlined in our hypothetical case applies equally to both. A person hoping to appeal a conviction for possession of cocaine in violation of state drug laws, for example, must present her appeal on an issue of law, not on an issue of fact. And, should the case reach the highest level of criminal law appeal in the state, the Texas Court of Criminal Appeals would hear and determine the outcome of the appeal. The Texas Supreme Court would have no jurisdictional standing since the case does not involve a matter of civil law.

Judicial Decision Making in Federal and State Appellate Courts

Many readers will recall from their studies of American government that American law is based on British common law. A fundamental feature of all common law systems is the doctrine of STARE DECISIS—or "let the decision stand"—commonly referred to as "precedent." When the United States Supreme Court delivers a ruling that is applicable to the states, state courts are required to follow the Court's decision and render decisions and opinions in state cases that are consistent with precedent Supreme Court cases. Furthermore, since the United States Constitution is "the supreme law of the land" (*United States Constitution*, Article VI), and the Supreme Court is the final interpreter of the law (*United States Constitution*, Article III), state laws deemed to be inconsistent with or repugnant to the United States Constitution are invalid (*FLETCHER V. PECK*, 1810).[425] Two United States Supreme Court cases, *FURMAN V. GEORGIA* (1972)[426] and *GREGG V. GEORGIA* (1976),[427] provide excellent examples of how Supreme Court precedent and the United States Constitution impact state court decision making. In *Furman*, the Court held that imposition of the death penalty violated the Eighth Amendment's ban against cruel and unusual punishment, and the Fourteenth Amendment's right to due process. Four years later, in *Gregg*, the Court abandoned *stare decisis*, reversed its previous decision in *Furman*, and reinstated the death penalty.

The *Furman* and *Gregg* decisions serve to highlight state court decision making in three ways. First, states may not deny their citizens the rights guaranteed them by the United States Constitution; however, states may, in their respective state constitutions, grant their citizens more rights as citizens of the state than those provided in the United States Constitution. Many state constitutions contain rights that are not contained in the United States Constitution as it is currently interpreted by the Supreme Court including the right to an efficient educational system (Texas), the right to physician-assisted suicide (Oregon), and the right against state criminal prosecution of patients prescribed and using medicinal marijuana (Colorado). When the Supreme Court handed down its decision in *Gregg*, pro-death penalty states were permitted to adopt statutes that allowed sentences of death; but, anti-death penalty states were not required to adopt similar statutes. Several state constitutions including Minnesota, West Virginia, and New York contain protections against cruel and unusual punishment,[428] and their state courts have ruled that imposition of the death penalty violates the state constitutional rights of their citizens. For this reason, 19 states currently do not have death as a punishment option. Conversely, when the Supreme Court issued its decision in *Furman*, all states including strong pro-death penalty states such as Texas were required to suspend and discontinue their practice of imposing death upon criminal defendants—regardless of existing state laws, rulings by state courts, or the sentiments of state voters and legislators. The national constitutional right against cruel and unusual punishment trumped any state interest in punishing people by death, and state courts and juries were bound to the *Furman* precedent—period.

Second, after the *Gregg* decision, pro-capital punishment states were allowed to write or rewrite their death penalty statutes on the condition their laws conformed to guidelines set forth in the *Gregg* opinion. One requirement outlined in *Gregg* was that all sentences of death must be automatically reviewed by the highest court in the state. Between 1977 (the year following the *Gregg* decision) and 2016, Texas juries imposed a sentence of death on 975 criminal defendants,[429] and as of May 15, 2017, a total of 542 of those sentences had been carried out by the state.[430] The total number of death sentences imposed by Texas juries may or may not reflect the actual number of automatic death sentence appeals reviewed by Texas Court of Criminal Appeals. Some individuals died on death row before their appeal reached the Court, and others were released from death row and their sentences converted to life imprisonment after post-*Gregg* United States Supreme Court decisions restricted the ability of states to carry out executions or impose death sentences in certain circumstances. Circumstances in which the Supreme Court has denied states the ability to execute prisoners include imposing death upon persons who do not understand the reason for or reality of their punishment (*Ford v. Wainwright*, 1986),[431] are diagnosed with mental retardation (*Atkins v. Virginia*, 2002),[432] or are under the age of 18 (*Roper v. Simmons*, 2005).[433] After post-*Gregg* Supreme Court rulings, Texas, regardless of the sentiments and preferences of its legislators, voters, judges, or juries, could not execute or sentence to death any person who qualified for federal constitutional protection due to mental illness, mental retardation, or age.

The sway of public opinion is the third way in which the *Furman* and *Gregg* decisions illuminate the processes of state court decision making. Texas is historically among the top three states with the highest number of death sentences imposed by juries, but it is also among the lowest in terms of successful appeals in death penalty cases.[434] The state's high rate of execution and low rate of successful appeal may well be attributed to the fact that Texas voters have historically been staunch proponents of the death penalty.[435] A 2012 survey conducted by the University of Texas at Austin and the *Texas Tribune* (UT/TT) revealed an overwhelming 73% of Texans were in favor of the death penalty compared to 21% of Texans opposed to the punishment.[436] The importance of Texas public opinion to understanding judicial decision making in the state is that, unlike judges serving in the federal judiciary, almost every Texas judge is elected by the voters of the state in partisan elections including all nine members of the Texas Court of Criminal Appeals and all nine members of the Texas Supreme Court. State high court judges do not hold life tenure as do federal judges; rather, they are elected by the voters in statewide partisan elections to six-year staggered terms, after which they are subject to reelection or defeat at the polls.

Lifetime appointment of federal judges was not an afterthought of the framers of the United States Constitution. The framers sought to remove federal judges as far as possible from the politics and political pressures of American life in order for them to have expanded opportunities to interpret law through the lens of reason, sound judgment, and objectivity. Legal scholars disagree on the degree to which public opinion influences United States Supreme Court decision making. However, history does demonstrate that the Court sometimes leads public opinion such as in the area of race equality and the famous 1954 decision, *Brown v. Board of Education*[437] that desegregated American public schools, and sometimes lags behind public opinion such as in the area of gender equality and the Court's 1971 decision in *Reed v. Reed*,[438] which finally deemed women "persons" under the Fourteenth Amendment—seven years after women were granted statutory equal rights by Congress in the Civil Rights Act of 1964. Regardless of the relative distance federal judges as a whole or individually have from public opinion, there is little doubt that the overall distance is astronomical when compared to state judges that are elected on partisan ballots by voters to six-year terms and subject to reelection and removal by statewide voting constituencies.

Understanding the correlation between public opinion and judicial decision making in Texas also offers insight into state politics and policy that might otherwise be hidden from immediate view. The 2012 UT/*TT* survey cited above, for example, revealed that 73% of Texans support the state's death penalty. However, since the Texas legislature passed a law in 2005 allowing juries the option to choose life in prison without parole in capital murder cases, the state's juries have been increasingly more reluctant to impose sentences of death in capital murder cases. Only three death penalty punishments were delivered by Texas juries in 2015—down from a high of 48 in 1999 and the lowest annual number of death penalty sentences issued in the state since the *Gregg v. Georgia* decision took effect in 1977.[439] At the same time, the number of life without parole sentences rose from four in 2006 to 102 in 2014.[440] The simultaneous decrease in Texas death penalty sentences and rise in sentences of life without parole may indicate Texas voters are not staunchly pro-death penalty *per se,* but rather desire to keep open to juries the option of choosing death as a punishment in cases that involve, for example, particularly heinous acts by the defendant or defendants that lack remorse and minimal chances of rehabilitation. The decline in death penalty sentences also means a reduction in Texas Court of Criminal Appeals caseload since life without parole sentences do not currently carry the requirement of automatic appeal as do death penalty sentences.

Figure 8.1

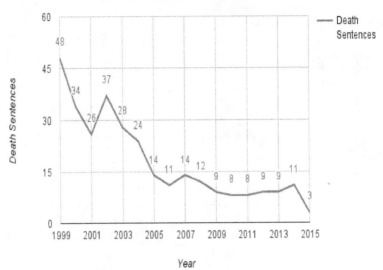

Source: Nicolson, Eric. "Texas Falls out of Love with the Death Penalty, Embraces Life without Parole." *Dallas Observer*, 17 Dec. 2015, www.dallasobserver.com/news/texas-falls-out-of-love-with-the-death-penalty-embraces-life-with out-parole-7860819.

153

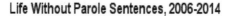

Figure 8.2

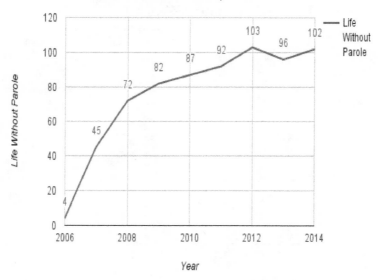

Life Without Parole Sentences, 2006-2014

Source: Nicolson, Eric. "Texas Falls out of Love with the Death Penalty, Embraces Life without Parole." *Dallas Observer*, 17 Dec. 2015, www.dallasobserver.com/news/texas-falls-out-of-love-with-the-death-penalty-embraces-life-with out-parole-7860819.

Texas Intermediate Courts of Appeals and Lower State District Courts

Below the bifurcated high court system in Texas are the state COURTS OF APPEALS and the STATE DISTRICT COURTS. The Texas Legislature has divided the state geographically into fourteen courts of appeals districts. Each district serves a number of Texas counties and contains one appellate court comprised of at least three justices—one chief justice and two justices. Today, a total of 80 justices serve on the fourteen state courts of appeals. State courts of appeals have appellate jurisdiction over both civil law and criminal law cases that come to them from the district or county courts.[441]

State district courts are trial courts of original jurisdiction. There are currently 467 state district courts in Texas. All courts of appeals and state district judges in Texas are elected in partisan elections by the voters in their respective districts. Courts of appeals judges are elected to six-year terms, and district court judges are elected to four-year terms.

Texas Constitutional and Statutory County Courts

The structure of the county court system in Texas is perhaps the most difficult level of the state judiciary to understand because it contains the division upon division of power discussed at length in previous chapters of this textbook. At the time the current Texas Constitution was written and ratified in 1876, county governments had perhaps the greatest potential for corruption and harm to citizens since they were the governments located closest to the people. The Texas Constitution therefore established a strong system of checks and balances by creating independent elective offices in each county.[442] Originally, the state Constitution provided for one county court in each of the state's 254 counties, consisting of elected "commissioners"[443] presided over by a county judge. The terms of office for members of the county commissioners' court including the county judge were only two years; but, in 1954, Texas voters ratified a state constitutional amendment increasing the terms of county court officials to four years.[444]

All Texas counties are divided into four precincts,[445] with one county commissioner elected from the voters of each precinct and a county judge elected at-large by the voters of the entire county. The county commissioners and the county judge serve together on the COUNTY COMMISSIONERS' COURT, with the COUNTY JUDGE presiding over the CONSTITUTIONAL COUNTY COURT. County commissioners' courts in Texas have some judicial power as outlined in Figure 3; however, since the state of Texas allows county governments a large degree of discretion over the duties and responsibilities their county governments hold as well as the ability to delegate power among county offices, the scope of judicial authority held by county commissioners' courts and county judges ranges considerably from county to county. In more rural counties, the commissioners' court and county judge continue to exercise a wide range of constitutional and statutory judicial authority; however, in more populous Texas counties, constitutional county courts and the county judge devote the vast majority of their time to running the day-to-day business of county government. At least 74 Texas counties have delegated, in whole or in part, the judicial duties of the county commissioners' court and county judge to STATUTORY COUNTY COURTS in order to allow the constitutional courts time to perform the executive and legislative functions of the county.[446] The main responsibilities of the county judges in these counties are to preside over the commissioners' court and serve as the county's chief administrator, and the primary tasks of the county commissioners' courts are to oversee the construction and maintenance of county roads and bridges and set the county budget and tax rate.[447] If we consider the most popular form of city government in Texas—the council-manager form, outlined in Chapter 4—we can deduce that in many Texas counties the executive and legislative roles of the constitutional county commissioners' court are similar to those performed by the city council for the city, and the role of the county judge as presiding officer over the county commissioners' courts is similar to that of the mayor presiding over the city council.

The Texas Constitution limits each county to a single constitutional county court.[448] Since constitutional county courts in the state's more populous counties now perform the executive and administrative functions of the county, the Texas Legislature has created statutory COUNTY COURTS AT-LAW to aid counties in their judicial functions. The creation and jurisdiction of every county court at-law is controlled by state statute; therefore, the respective jurisdiction of each county court at-law varies considerably from county to county.[449] As of 2017, the Texas legislature has created 243 statutory county courts at-law serving 88 Texas counties (Figure 3). In general, county courts at-law handle all civil and criminal cases that would otherwise be handled by the constitutional county courts and have concurrent original jurisdiction with state district courts over civil matters involving possible judgments ranging from $200 to $200,000 (Figure 3). County courts at-law also have appellate jurisdiction over cases appealed from municipal and justice of the peace courts.[450]

Municipal Courts and Justice of the Peace Courts

The Texas legislature has created at least one MUNICIPAL COURT for every incorporated city in Texas, and larger cities have more than one, based on a city's population and need.[451] Municipal courts have original jurisdiction over cases concerning city laws and ordinances relating to fire safety, zoning, public health, sanitation, and city traffic laws. Most Texas municipal court judges are selected by the city council rather than elected by the city's voters. Municipal court judges may issue search or arrest warrants but generally do not have civil law jurisdiction except in cases concerning owners of dangerous dogs.[452] JUSTICE OF THE PEACE COURTS have original jurisdiction over minor misdemeanor criminal offenses and minor civil matters including small claims; may issue search or arrest warrants; and may serve as the coroner in counties where there is no provision for a medical examiner. The Texas Constitution requires each county to establish between one and eight justice of the peace precincts depending upon the population of the county.[453]

Figure 8.3

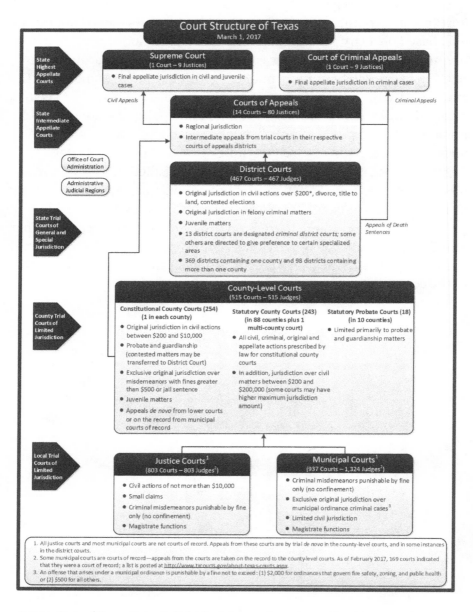

Source: *State of Texas, Texas Judicial Branch*. www.txcourts.gov/about-texas-courts.aspx.
Accessed 17 Nov. 2017.

Conclusion

The structure of the Texas judiciary is widely considered one of the most complex judicial structures in the world. Multiple divisions of judicial power that include a bifurcated high court system and county judicial structure divided between constitutional courts and statutory courts are exacerbated by constitutional requirements that almost all state judges—ranging from those serving on the two high courts to the 803 Texas justice of the peace courts—be elected in partisan elections by Texas voters.

Key Terms

jurisdiction

appellate jurisdiction

criminal law

bifurcated high court

Texas Court of Criminal Appeals

Fletcher v. Peck

Gregg v. Georgia

state district courts

county judges

statutory county courts

municipal courts

original jurisdiction

en banc

civil law

Texas Supreme Court

stare decisis

Furman v. Georgia

state courts of appeals

county commissioners' courts

constitutional county courts

county courts at-law

justice of the peace courts

END NOTES

Introduction
p. 15
1. "Official Texas Historical Markers." *Texas Historical Commission,* July 2015, www.thc.texas.gov/public/upload/forms/thc-historical-markers-factsheet.pdf.

Unit 1
Chapter 1
p. 19
2. "American Indians: A story told for thousands of years." *The Story of Texas (online),* The Bullock Museum, www.thestoryoftexas.com/discover/campfire-stories/native-americans. Accessed 3 Nov. 2017.

p. 20
3. Birzer, Dedra McDonald. "Esteban (?–1539)." *BlackPast.org: An Online Reference Guide to African American History,* www.blackpast.org/gah/esteban-1539. Accessed 3 Nov. 2017.
4. Donoghue, David. "Coronado Expedition." *Handbook of Texas Online,* Texas State Historical Association, 12 June 2010, https://tshaonline.org/handbook/online/articles/upcpt.
5. Weddle, Robert S. "La Salle's Texas Settlement." *Handbook of Texas Online,* Texas State Historical Association, 30 Oct. 2011, https://tshaonline.org/handbook/online/articles/uel07.
6. "Angelina." *Women in Texas History: Ruthe Winegarten Memorial Foundation for Texas Women's History,* www.womenintexashistory.org/bios/. Accessed 3 Nov. 2017.

p. 21
7. De León, Arnoldo. "Mexican Americans." *Handbook of Texas Online,* Texas State Historical Association, 26 Jan. 2017, https://tshaonline.org/handbook/online/articles/pqmue.
8. Ibid.
9. Interestingly, the name "Barataria" derives from a fictional isle that

was awarded by some noblemen to Sancho Panza as part of a prank in Part II of Cervantes' *Don Quixote*, published in 1615. www.online-literature.com/cervantes/don_quixote/. Accessed 3 Nov. 2017.
10. Harris, Gaylord Warren. "Lafitte, Jean." *Handbook of Texas Online*, Texas State Historical Association, 4 Feb. 2014, https://tshaonline.org/handbook/online/articles/fla12.
11. Bell, Shane. "The War of 1812: Privateers, Plunder, & Profiteering." *The National Archives: The Text Message Blog*, U. S. National Archives, 3 June 2013, https://text-message.blogs.archives.gov/2013/06/03/the-war-of-1812-privateers-plunder-profiteering/.

p. 22
12. Warren, Harris Gaylord. "Lafitte, Jean." *Handbook of Texas Online*, Texas State Historical Association, 4 Feb. 2014, https://tshaonline.org/handbook/online/articles/fla12.
13. Hoffman, Paul E. *A History of Louisiana before 1813*. Louisiana State University Bookstore, 1996, p. 90.

p. 23
14. "Treaty of San Ildefonso." *The Napolean Series*, Sept. 2000, https://napoleon-series.org/research/government/diplomatic/c_ildefonso.html.
15. Greenspan, Jesse. "Eight Things You May Not Know about the Louisiana Purchase." *History in the Headlines,* The History Channel, 30 Apr. 2013, www.history.com/news/8-things-you-may-not-know-about-the-louisiana-purchase.
16. Ibid.

p. 24
17. Warren, Harris Gaylord. "Gutierrez-Magee Expedition." *Handbook of Texas Online*, Texas State Historical Association, 15 June 2010, https://tshaonline.org/handbook/online/articles/qyg01.
18. Warren, Harris Gaylord. "Long Expedition." *Handbook of Texas Online*, Texas State Historical Association, 25 July 2017, https://tshaonline.org/handbook/online/articles/qyl01.

p. 25

19. "RootsWeb." *Ancestry,* http://home.rootsweb.ancestry.com. Accessed 3 Nov. 2017.
20. Ibid.
21. "Jane Wilkinson Long (1798–1880) and Kian." *Women in Texas History: Ruthe Winegarten Memorial Foundation for Texas Women's History,* www.womenintexashistory.org/bios/. Accessed 3 Nov. 2017.
22. Rice, Harvey and Claudia Feldman. "Texas Pioneer Jane Long Gave Birth in Brutal Winter, Defended Fort." *Beaumont Enterprise,* 19 Sept. 2016, www.beaumontenterprise.com/news/article/Texas-pioneer-Jane-Long-gave-birth-in-brutal-9231609.php.
23. Ibid.
24. Ibid.

p. 26
25. "A Guide to the Baron de Bastrop Papers in the Natchez Trace Collection." *Briscoe Center for American History*, University of Texas at Austin, https://www.lib.utexas.edu/taro/utcah/00389/cah-00389.html. Accessed 3 Nov. 2017.
26. Gracy, David B., II. "Austin, Moses." *Handbook of Texas Online,* Texas State Historical Association, 9 May 2016, https://tshaonline.org/handbook/online/articles/fau12.
27. Moore, Richard W. "Bastrop, Baron De." *Handbook of Texas Online*, Texas State Historical Association, 9 May 2016, https://www.tshaonline.org/handbook/online/articles/fbaae.

p. 27
28. Ibid.
29. Gracy, David B., II. "Austin, Moses." *Handbook of Texas Online,* Texas State Historical Association, 9 May 2016, https://tshaonline.org/handbook/online/articles/fau12.
30. Long, Christopher. "Old Three Hundred." *Handbook of Texas Online*, Texas State Historical Association, 10 May 2016, https://tshaonline.org/handbook/online/articles/um001.
31. Ibid.

Chapter 2
p. 29
32. Long, Christopher. "Old Three Hundred." *Handbook of Texas*

163

Online, Texas State Historical Association, 10 May 2016, https://tshaonline.org/handbook/online/articles/um001.
33. "Irish Texans." *Texas Almanac,* Texas State Historical Association, https://texasalmanac.com/topics/culture/irish/irish-texans. Accessed 3 Nov. 2017.
34. Long, Christopher. "Old Three Hundred." *Handbook of Texas Online,* Texas State Historical Association, 10 May 2016, https://tshaonline.org/handbook/online/articles/um001.
35. Ibid.
36. Ibid.

p. 30
37. Ibid.
38. "Research in the Lonestar State: Immigration to Texas." *Lonestar Genealogy,* www.lonestargenealogy.com/courses/texas/migration.html. Accessed 6 Nov. 2017.
39. "African Americans." *Bullock Museum,* Bullock Texas State History Museum, https://www.thestoryoftexas.com/discover/campfire-stories/african-americans. Accessed 6 Nov. 2017.
40. Ibid.
41. Ibid.
42. Ginsberg, Benjamin, et al. *We the People: An Introduction to American Politics.* 9th ed., Texas edition, W. W. Norton & Co., 2013, p. 781.

p. 31
43. Dulaney, Marvin W. "African Americans." *Handbook of Texas Online,* Texas State Historical Association, 25 July 2016, https://tshaonline.org/handbook/online/articles/pkaan.
44. Ibid.
45. "Why Dallas?" *Texas Monthly,* Dec. 1973, https://www.texasmonthly.com/articles/why-dallas/.
46. McDavid, Carol, et al. "Urban Archeology and the Pressures of Gentrification: Claiming, Naming, and Negotiating 'Freedom' in Freedmen's Town, Houston." *Texas Archaeological Society 79,* 2008, http://freedmanstownarchaeology.rice.edu/reports/McDavid_et_al%20_BTAS_79_2008.pdf.

47. Acosta, Teresa Palomo. "Juneteenth." *Handbook of Texas Online,* Texas State Historical Association, 6 Oct. 2017, https://www.tshaonline.org/handbook/online/articles/lkj01.
48. Gates, Henry Louis, Jr. "What is Juneteenth? The First Juneteenth." The African Americans: Many Rivers to Cross, *Public Broadcasting System (PBS)*, 2013, www.pbs.org/wnet/african-americans-many-rivers-to-cross/history/what-is-juneteenth/
49. Ibid.

p. 32
50. Ibid.
51. Ibid.
52. Acosta, Teresa Palomo. "Juneteenth." *Handbook of Texas Online,* Texas State Historical Association, 6 Oct. 2017, https://www.tshaonline.org/handbook/online/articles/lkj01.
53. Ibid.
54. "National Registry of Juneteenth Organizations and Supporters." *Juneteenth*, www.juneteenth.com/worldwide.htm. Accessed 6 Nov. 2017.
55. Whitehurst, Katie. "Spanish Colonial: 1689–1821." *Texas Our Texas*, Texas PBS/Humanities Texas/The Summerlee Foundation, http://texasourtexas.texaspbs.org/the-eras-of-texas/spanish-colonial/. Accessed 6 Nov. 2017.
56. Ibid.

p. 33
57. Ibid.
58. "Canary Islanders." *Handbook of Texas Online,* Texas State Historical Association, 9 May 2016, https://tshaonline.org/handbook/online/articles/poc01.
59. Ibid.
60. de la Teja, Jesús F. "San Fernando de Bexar." *Handbook of Texas Online,* Texas State Historical Association, 9 May 2016, https://www.tshaonline.org/handbook/online/articles/hvs16.
61. Ibid.
62. "Canary Islanders." *Handbook of Texas Online,* Texas State Historical Association, 9 May 2016, https://tshaonline.org/handbook/online/articles/poc01.

63. Haneveer, Victoria. "How the Cuisine of the Canary Islands Influenced Tex-Mex." *Houstonia,* Saga City Media, 19 Aug. 2016, https://www.houstoniamag.com/articles/2016/8/19/how-the-cuisine-of-the-canary-islands-is-related-to-tex-mex.

p. 34
64. Acosta, Teresa Palomo. "María Gertrudis Pérez Cordero Cassiano." *Women in Texas History: Ruthe Winegarten Memorial Foundation for Texas History,* www.womenintexashistory.org/audio/cassiano. Accessed 6 Nov. 2017.
65. Ibid.
66. Weiser, Kathy. "Hutchinson County—Panhandle Frontier." *Legends of America,* June 2013, https://www.legendsofamerica.com/tx-hutchinsoncounty.html.

p. 35
67. Weiser, Kathy. "Adobe Walls—Buffalo and Battles." *Legends of America,* June 2016, https:// www.legendsofamerica.com/tx-adobewalls.html.
68. Ibid.
69. Ibid.
70. Haley, James L. "Red River War." *Handbook of Texas Online,* Texas State Historical Association, 12 Oct. 2016, https://tshaonline.org/handbook/online/articles/qdr02.
71. Ibid.

p. 36
72. Hosmer, Brian C. "Parker, Quanah." *Handbook of Texas Online,* Texas State Historical Association, 28 March 2016, http://www.tshaonline.org/handbook/online/articles/fpa28.
73. Ibid.
74. Ibid.

p. 37
75. Ibid.
76. Ibid.
77. "American Indians in Texas." *Texas Almanac,* Texas State Historical Association,

http://texasalmanac.com/topics/culture/american-indian/american-indian. Accessed 6 Nov. 2017.

78. Dickerson, W. E. S. "Indian Reservations." *Handbook of Texas Online,* Texas State Historical Association, 15 June 2010, https://tshaonline.org/handbook/online/articles/bpi01.

79. Dickerson, W. E. S. "Indian Reservations." *Handbook of Texas Online,* Texas State Historical Association, 15 June 2010, https://tshaonline.org/handbook/online/articles/bpi01.

p. 38

80. Ibid.

81. Ibid.

82. Jordan, Terry G. "Germans." *Handbook of Texas Online,* Texas State Historical Association, 7 Mar. 2016, https://tshaonline.org/handbook/online/articles/png02.

83. Malsch, Brownson. "Indianola, TX." *Handbook of Texas Online,* Texas State Historical Association, 1 May 2017, https://tshaonline.org/handbook/online/articles/hvi11.

84. Jordan, Terry G. "Germans." *Handbook of Texas Online,* Texas State Historical Association, 7 Mar. 2017, https://tshaonline.org/handbook/online/articles/png02.

85. Fehrenbach, T. R. "San Antonio, TX." *Handbook of Texas Online,* Texas State Historical Association, 30 Mar. 2017, https://tshaonline.org/handbook/online/articles/hds02.

p. 39

86. Malsch, Brownson. "Indianola, TX." *Handbook of Texas Online,* Texas State Historical Association, 1 May 2017, https://tshaonline.org/handbook/online/articles/hvi11.

87. Biesele, Rudolph L. "German Attitude Toward the Civil War." *Handbook of Texas Online,* Texas State Historical Association, 8 Mar. 2011, https://tshaonline.org/handbook/online/articles/png01.

88. Ibid.

89. Lich, Glen E. "Comfort, Texas." *Handbook of Texas Online,* Texas State Historical Association, 30 June 2010, https://tshaonline.org/handbook/online/articles/hjc16.

90. Plocheck, Robert. "Czech Texans." *Texas Almanac,* Texas State Historical Association,

http://texasalmanac.com/topics/culture/czech/czech-texans. Accessed
6 Nov. 2017.

p. 40
91. Machann, Clinton. "Czechs." *Handbook of Texas Online,* Texas
State Historical Association, 1 Apr. 2016,
https://tshaonline.org/handbook/online/articles/plc02.
92. Ibid.
93. Ibid.
94. "Irish Texans." *Texas Almanac* , Texas State Historical Association,
http://texasalmanac.com/topics/culture/irish/irish-texans. Accessed 6
Nov. 2017.
95. Ibid.
96. Moody, Joan. "San Antonio's Irish Roots Are Deep." *San Antonio
Express-News*, Hearst, 12 Mar. 2010,
www.mysanantonio.com/news/article/San-Antonio-s-Irish-roots-are-
deep-788955.php.
97. Robert Plocheck. "Scot/Scotch-Irish." *Texas Almanac,* Texas State
Historical Association,
http://texasalmanac.com/topics/culture/scotscotch-irish/scotscotch-
irish. Accessed 6 Nov. 2017.
98. Ibid.

p. 41
99. "Research in the Lonestar State: Immigration to Texas." *Lonestar
Geneology*,
www.lonestargenealogy.com/courses/texas/migration.html. Accessed
6 Nov. 2017.
100. Ibid.
101. Ibid.
102. "French." *Handbook of Texas Online,* Texas State Historical
Association, 25 Nov. 2013,
https://tshaonline.org/handbook/online/articles/pmf01.
103. Williams, Amelia W. "Castro, Henri." *Handbook of Texas Online,*
Texas State Historical Association, 29 Feb. 2016,
https://tshaonline.org/handbook/online/articles/fca93.
104. Ibid.
105. Williams, Amelia W. "Castro, Henri." *Handbook of Texas Online,*

Texas State Historical Association, 29 Feb. 2016,
https://tshaonline.org/handbook/online/articles/fca93.

p. 42
106. McCorkle, James L., Jr. "Los Adaes." *Handbook of Texas Online,*
Texas State Historical Association, 15 June 2010,
https://tshaonline.org/handbook/online/articles/nfl01.
107. Ibid.
108. Galan, Francis. "Los Adaes, the Final Years: Evacuation and
Resettlement." *Texas Beyond History*, University of Texas at Austin,
College of Liberal Arts,
https://www.texasbeyondhistory.net/adaes/final.html. Accessed 7
Nov. 2017.
109. Ibid.
110. Ibid.
111. Ibid.
112. McDonald, Archie P. "Nacogdoches, Texas." *Handbook of Texas
Online,* Texas State Historical Association, 15 June 2010,
https://tshaonline.org/handbook/online/articles/hdn01.

p. 43
113. Galan, Francis. "Los Adaes, the Final Years: Evacuation and
Resettlement." *Texas Beyond History*, University of Texas at Austin,
College of Liberal Arts,
https://www.texasbeyondhistory.net/adaes/final.html. Accessed 7
Nov. 2017.
114. Ibid.
115. "Antonio Gil Y'Barbo." *Nacogdoches County Chamber of
Commerce*, www.nacogdoches.org/page.php? cat=history&id=5.
Accessed 7 Nov. 2017.
116. Blake, Robert Bruce. "Ibarvo, Antonio Gil." *Handbook of Texas
Online,* Texas State Historical Association, 26 July 2017,
https://tshaonline.org/handbook/online/articles/fib01.

Chapter 3
p. 45
117. "The Nine Flags at the Historic Town Center in Historic
Nacogdoches." *Pictures of Historic Nacogdoches*, www.pictures-of-

169

historic-nacogdoches.com/023nineflags.html. Accessed 7 Nov. 2017.

118. Diaz, Joy. "In Laredo, It's Seven Flags Over Texas: The Republic of the Rio Grande was its own short-lived country on the Texas border." *Texas Standard,* Moody College of Communication at the University of Texas at Austin, 22 Oct. 2015, www.texasstandard.org/ stories/in-laredo-its-seven-flags-over-texas/.

p. 46

119. Hardin, Stephen L. "Gonzales, Battle of." *Handbook of Texas Online,* Texas State Historical Association, 30 June 2016, https://tshaonline.org/handbook/online/articles/qeg03.

120. Ibid.

121. Lindley, Thomas Ricks. "Gonzales Come and Take It Cannon." *Handbook of Texas Online,* Texas State Historical Association, 11 July 2016, https://tshaonline.org/handbook/online/articles/qvg01.

122. "Struggle for Mexican Independence." *History*, A+E Networks, 2010, www.history.com/topics/mexico/struggle-for-mexican-independence.

p. 47

123. "Spain Accepts Mexican Independence." *History*, A+E Networks, 2010, http://www.history.com/this-day-in-history/spain-accepts-mexican-independence.

124. "*Cinco de Mayo.*" *History*, A+E Networks, 2010, http://www.history.com/this-day-in-history/cinco-de-mayo.

p.48

125. Ibid.

126. "The Mexican Campaign, 1862–1867." *Napoleon*, Fondation Napoléon, https://www.napoleon.org/en/history-of-the-two-empires/timelines/the-mexican-campaign-1862-1867. Accessed 7 Nov. 2017.

127. Leopold, Todd. "5 Things to Know about Cinco de Mayo." *CNN*, 4 May 2016, www.cnn.com/2015/05/04/living/feat-cinco-de-mayo-5-things/.

128. Ibid.

129. Ibid.

130. Tomkiw, Lydia. "Cinco de Mayo: How Is the Holiday Celebrated in

Mexico? History, Facts and Misconceptions about May 5."
International Business Times, Newsweek Media Group, 5 May 2016,
www.ibtimes.com/cinco-de-mayo-how-holiday-celebrated-mexico-history-facts-misconceptions-about-may-5-2363978.
131. "Spain Accepts Mexican Independence." *History,* A+E Networks,
2010, www.history.com/this-day-in-history/spain-accepts-mexican-independence.
132. Ibid.

p. 49
133. Hyman, Carolyn. "Iturbide, Agustin de." *Handbook of Texas
Online,* Texas State Historical Association, 5 May 2016,
https://tshaonline.org/handbook/online/articles/fit01.
134. Olvera, Jose Pablo. "Guadalupe Victoria: Mexico's First President:
Independence Hero." *Inside Mexico,* 22 July 2015, https://www.inside-mexico.com/guadalupe-victoria-mexicos-first-president/.
135. Rivera, Alicia. "Guerrero, Vicente (1783–1831)." *BlackPast,*
www.blackpast.org/gah/guerrero-Vicente-1783-1831. Accessed 7 Nov.
2017.
136. Ibid.
137. "Vicente Guerrero: An Inventory of His Collection." *Texas Archival
Resources Online*, The Nettie Lee Benson Latin American Collection,
The University of Texas at Austin,
http://www.lib.utexas.edu/taro/utlac/00026/lac-00026.html.
Accessed 7 Nov. 2017.
138. McKay, S. S. "Constitution of Coahuila and Texas." *Handbook of
Texas Online,* Texas State Historical Association, 12 June 2010,
https://tshaonline.org/handbook/online/articles/ngc01.

p. 50
139. "The Alamo." *History,* A+E Networks, 2010,
www.history.com/topics/alamo.
140. Ibid.
141. Covington, Carolyn Callaway. "Runaway Scrape." *Handbook of
Texas Online,* Texas State Historical Association, 31 July 2016,
https://tshaonline.org/handbook/online/articles/pfr01.
142. Ibid.
143. Ibid.

p. 51

144. "Battle of San Jacinto." *History*, A+E Networks, 2009, www.history.com/topics/battle-of-san-jacinto.

145. Covington, Carolyn Callaway. "Runaway Scrape." *The Handbook of Texas Online,* Texas State Historical Association, 31 July 2016, https://tshaonline.org/handbook/online/articles/pfr01.

146. Harris, Trudier. "The Yellow Rose of Texas: The Ironic Origins of a Popular Song." *BlackPast*, www.blackpast.org/perspectives/yellow-rose-texas-ironic-origins-state-song. Accessed 7 Nov. 2017.

147. Ibid.

148. Garner, Claude W. *Sam Houston: Texas Giant.* Naylor Co., 1969.

p. 52

149. Whitelaw, Mark. "In Search of the Yellow Rose of Texas." *Sons of DeWitt Colony Texas,* www.tamu.edu/faculty/ccbn/dewitt/adp/archives/yellowrose/yelrose.html. Accessed 8 Nov. 2017.

150. Ibid.

151. "Emily D. West." *Women in Texas: Ruthe Winegarten Memorial Foundation for Texas Women's History,* www.womenintexashistory.org/bios/#EmilyWest. Accessed 8 Nov. 2017.

152. Ericson, Joe E. "Constitution of the Republic of Texas." *Handbook of Texas Online,* Texas State Historical Association, 2 Mar. 2016, https://tshaonline.org/handbook/online/articles/mhc01.

p. 53

153. "The Archives War," *Texas State Library and Archives Commission* https://www.tsl.texas.gov/treasures/republic/archwar/archwar.html. Accessed 8 Nov. 2017.

p. 54

154. Buenger, Walter L. "Secession." *Handbook of Texas Online,* Texas State Historical Association, 8 Mar. 2011, https://tshaonline.org/handbook/online/articles/mgs02.

p. 55
155. Bishop, Curtis. "Coke-Davis Controversy." *Handbook of Texas Online,* Texas State Historical Association, 18 Jan. 2017, https://tshaonline.org/handbook/online/articles/mqc01.
156. *Ex parte Rodriguez.* 39 Tex. 705. 1874.

p. 56
157. "Travis Guards and Rifles." *Handbook of Texas Online*, Texas State Historical Association, 15 June 2010, https://tshaonline.org/handbook/online/articles/qjt03; See also Gately, Staff Sgt. John. "The long, proud history of the Texas State Guard." *Texas Military Department*, https://tmd.texas.gov/the-long-proud-history-of-the-texas-state-guard. Accessed 8 Nov. 2017.
158. Bishop, Curtis. "Coke-Davis Controversy." *Handbook of Texas Online,* Texas State Historical Association, 18 Jan. 2017, https://tshaonline.org/handbook/online/articles/mqc01.

p. 57
159. Elazar, Daniel J. *American Federalism: A View from the States.* 1966. HarperCollins, 1984.
160. Ibid, p. 90.
161. Madison, James. *Federalist Papers,* No. 10 and 51.
162. Madison, James. *Federalist Papers,* No. 10.

p. 58
163. National Center for Charitable Statistics. "Profiles of Individual Charitable Contributions by State: 2013." *Urban Institute*, 10 Feb. 2016, https://www.urban.org/research/publication/profiles-individual-charitable-contributions-state-2013.
164. Members of the Texas Legislature are paid an annual salary of $7,200. "2015 State Legislator Compensation." *National Conference of State Legislators*, 14 May 2015, www.ncsl.org/research/about-state-legislatures/2015-state-legislator-compensation.aspx.
165. Ginsberg, Benjamin, et al. *We the People: An Introduction to American Politics.* 9th ed., Texas edition, 2013, W. W. Norton & Co., p. 768.

p. 59
166. Ibid., pp. 768–769.
167. Ibid., p. 773.

p. 60
168. Ibid., p. 781.
169. Linsley, Judith. "African-American Neighborhoods Grew Where the People Worked." *Stephen F. Austin University*, May 2014, www.sfasu.edu/heritagecenter/9191.asp.
170. DiSalvo, Daniel. "The Great Reverse Migration: African-Americans Are Abandoning the Northern Cities That Have Failed Them." *Pittsburgh Post-Gazette*, 30 Sept. 2012, www.post-gazette.com/opinion/Op-Ed/2012/09/30/The-Great-Reverse-Migration-African-Americans-are-abandoning-the-Northern-cities-that-have-failed-them/stories/201209300228.
171. Ibid.
172. Ibid.
173. "Texas Black Demographics." *Black Demographics*, http://blackdemographics.com/states/texas/. Accessed 9 Nov. 2017.
174. *United States Census Bureau*, U.S. Department of Commerce, https://www.census.gov/quickfacts. Accessed 9 Nov. 2017.

p. 61
175. Ibid.
176. Collin County Republican Party. "African Americans and Texas Politics." *Collin County Republican Party*, 27 July 2009, https://www.collincountygop.org/news/african-americans-and-texas-politics.
177. De León, Arnoldo. "Mexican Americans." *Handbook of Texas Online*, Texas State Historical Association, 26 Jan. 2017, https://tshaonline.org/handbook/online/articles/pqmue.
178. Murphy, Ryan, and Matt Stiles. "Census 2010 Interactive Map: Texas Population By Race, Hispanic Origin." *The Texas Tribune*, 4 Jan. 2012, https://www.texastribune.org/library/data/census-2010.
179. *United States Census Bureau*, U.S. Department of Commerce, http://www.census.gov/quickfacts. Accessed 9 Nov. 2017.
180. "The Texas Politics Project: Latino Elected Officials in Texas, 1974–2003." *The Texas Politics Project*, University of Texas at Austin,

https://texaspolitics.utexas.edu/archive/html/vce/features/0503_04/l
atinos.html. Accessed 9 Nov. 2017.

181. Potter, Lloyd B., and Nazrul Hoque. "Texas Population Projections
2010 to 2050." *Texas Demographic Center*, Office of the State
Demographer/Texas State Data Center, 2014,
http://demographics.texas.gov/Resources/Publications/2014/2014-11
_ProjectionBrief.pdf.

p. 62

182. *United States Census Bureau*, U.S. Department of Commerce,
http://www.census.gov/quickfacts. Accessed 9 Nov. 2017.

183. Potter, Lloyd B., and Nazrul Hoque. "Texas Population
Projections, 2010 to 2050." *Texas Demographic Center,* Office of the
State Demographer/Texas State Data Center, 2014,
http://demographics.texas.gov/Resources/Publications/2014/2014-11
_ProjectionBrief.pdf.

184. "Census of Population and Housing." *United States Census
Bureau*, U.S. Department of Commerce,
https://www.census.gov/prod/cen2010. Accessed 9 Nov. 2017.

185. Ibid.

186. Plocheck, Robert. "American Indians in Texas." *Texas Almanac,*
Texas State Historical Association,
https://texasalmanac.com/topics/culture/american-indian/american-i
ndian. Accessed 9 Nov. 2017.

187. "The American Indian and Alaska Native Population: 2010."
United States Census Bureau, U.S. Department of Commerce,
https://www.census.gov/prod/cen2010/briefs/c2010br-10.pdf.
Accessed 9 Nov. 2017.

188. Ibid.

189. *Texas Constitution*. Article I, Bill of Rights, Sect. 3a.

p. 63

190. Daniel, Theresa. "How Texas Led the Women's Suffrage
Movement." *Dallas Morning News*, Aug. 2016,
www.dallasnews.com/opinion/commentary/2016/08/25/texas-lead-w
omens-suffrage-movement.

191. Taylor, A. Elizabeth. "Woman Suffrage." *The Handbook of Texas
Online*, Texas State Historical Association, 18 Aug. 2017,

https://tshaonline.org/handbook/online/articles/viw01.

192. Daniel, Theresa. "How Texas Led the Women's Suffrage Movement." *Dallas Morning News*, Aug. 2016, www.dallasnews.com/opinion/commentary/2016/08/25/texas-lead-womens-suffrage-movement.

193. Ibid.

194. Ibid.

p. 64

195. "Timeline." *Women in Texas History*, Ruthe Winegarten Memorial Foundation for Texas Women's History, www.womenintexashistory.org/timeline/. Accessed 9 Nov. 2017.

196. Farenthold was defeated by Dolph Brisco in her run for Texas governor in 1972.

197. Barbara Jordan was the first African-American since 1883 to serve in the Texas Senate; the first African-American women and (along with Andrew Young of Georgia) African-American Southerner to be elected to the U. S. Congress since Reconstruction; the first woman and the first African-American to deliver the keynote address to the Democratic National Convention; and the first African-American buried in the Texas State Cemetery in Austin. See: "History of Barbara Jordan." *University of Texas Division of Diversity and Community Engagement: Barbar Jordan Statue Project*, University of Texas at Austin, http://diversity.utexas.edu/barbarajordanstatue/history-of-barbara-jordan/. Accessed 9 Nov. 2017.

198. "Texas Equal Rights Amendment." *Texas Law: Frances Tarleton "Sissy" Farenthold, A Noble Citizen*, University of Texas at Austin, https://law.utexas.edu/farenthold/state/texas-equal-rights-amendment/. Accessed 9 Nov. 2017.

199. Ibid.

p. 65

200. Senator Bensen vacated the office to become U. S. Treasury Secretary under President Bill Clinton.

201. Senator Cruz subsequently changed political party affiliation from the Tea Party to the Republican Party.

Unit 2

Chapter 4

p. 70

202. The Confederate States of America during the Civil War also ensured states primary government power.

p. 72

203. *McCulloch v. Maryland.* 17 U.S. 316. 1819.

p. 73

204. Large portions of this segment of "For the Record" was taken from:
Davis, Terri B. "The Rhetoric of Political Conservativism in the Post-Reagan Era." *Open Journal of Political Science*, Vol. 6, No. 2, April 2016.
205. Witherspoon, John. cited in Ford, W.C., et al. (eds.), 1907. *Journals of the Continental Congress 1774-1789*, 34 volumes. Library of Congress, pp. 1103–1104.
206. Storing, Herbert J. *The Complete Anti-Federalist.* Vol. 2. University of Chicago Press, 1981, p. 207.

p. 74

207. Henry, Patrick, cited in Storing, Herbert J. *The Complete Anti-Federalist.* Vol. 2, University of Chicago Press, 1981, p. 212.
208. Storing, Herbert J. *The Complete Anti-Federalist.* Vol. 2,University of Chicago Press, Vol. 2, pp. 19–82.
209. Ibid., pp. 3–83.
210. Ibid., pp. 255–256.
211. "Hampden" Essays. 1819. Reprinted in Gunther, Gerald, editor. *John Marshall's Defense of* McCulloch v. Maryland. Stanford University Press, 1969, p. 140.
212. A Virginian's "Amphictyon" Essays. 1819. Reprinted in Gunther, Gerald, editor. *John Marshall's Defense of* McCulloch v. Maryland. Stanford University Press, 1969, pp. 56–57.

p. 75

213. Gunther, Gerald, editor. *John Marshall's Defense of* McCulloch v. Maryland. Stanford University Press, 1969.

214. Marshall's "A Friend to the Union" Essays. April 24–28, 1819. Reprinted in Gunther, Gerald, editor. *John Marshall's Defense of* McCulloch v. Maryland. Stanford University Press, 1969, pp. 78–105, citation p. 84.

215. *Gibbons v. Ogden.* 22 U.S. 1. 1824.

216. *National Labor Relations Board v. Jones & Laughlin Steel Corporation.* 301 U. S. 1. 1937.

217. *Heart of Atlanta Motel v. U. S.* 379 U. S. 241. 1964.

p. 76

218. *U. S. v. Lopez.* 514 U. S. 549. 1995.

219. *Printz v. U. S.* 521 U. S. 898. 1997.

220. *U. S. v. Morrison.* 529 U. S. 598. 2000.

221. Under general revenue sharing programs, federal funds are distributed to state and local governments with very few restrictions on how and where the funds are spent.

222. "American Federalism." *American Government.* Ch. 3, Rice University, 2016.

p. 77

223. "Federal Grants to State and Local Governments." *Congressional Budget Office*, 5 Mar. 2013, https://www.cbo.gov/publication/43967.

224. Mach, Annie L., and C. Stephen Redhead. "Federal Funding for Health Insurance Exchanges." Congressional Research Service, a Division of the Library of Congress, *Federation of American Scientists*, 29 Oct. 2014, https://fas.org/sgp/crs/misc/R43066.pdf.

225. Duncombe, William, et al. "The No Child Left Behind Act: Have Federal Funds Been Left Behind?" *Center for Policy Research*, The Maxwell School of Public Administration, Syracuse University, September 2006, http://cpr.maxwell.syr.edu/efap/Publications/costing_out.pdf.

226. "Fact Sheet: Task Force for Faith-Based and Community Initiatives." *United States Department of Justice Archive*, https://www.justice.gov/archive/fbci/about.html. Accessed 10 Nov. 2017.

227. Dwyer, Devin. "Faith-Based Debate: Obama Signs Order on Funds for Churches." *ABC News*, 18 Nov. 2010, http://abcnews.go.com/Politics/president-obama-executive-order-fait

h-based- initiative-church/story?id=12180146.

228. "Federal Grants to State and Local Governments." *Congressional Budget Office*, 5 Mar. 2013, https://www.cbo.gov/publication/43967.

229. Ibid.

230. Ibid.

p. 78

231. Ibid.

232. Ibid.

p. 79

233. "History of Texas Counties." *Texas Association of Counties*, https://www.county.org/texas-county-government/county-govt-structure/Pages/History.aspx. Accessed 10 Nov. 2017.

234. Ibid.

235. Ibid.

236. "County Commissioner." *Texas Association of Counties*, https://www.county.org/texas-county-government/texas-county-officials/Pages/County-Commissioner.aspx. Accessed 10 Nov. 2017.

p. 81

237. Blodgett, Terrell. "Home Rule Charters." *Handbook of Texas Online*, Texas State Historical Association, 15 June 2010, https://tshaonline.org/handbook/online/articles/mvhek.

238. "General Law City Law and Legal Definition." *USLegal*, https://definitions.uslegal.com/g/general-law-city/. Accessed 10 Nov. 2017.

239. Blodgett, Terrell. "Home Rule Charters." *Handbook of Texas Online*, Texas State Historical Association, 15 June 2010, https://tshaonline.org/handbook/online/articles/mvhek.

240. "Local Government Authority." *National League of Cities*, http://www.nlc.org/local-government-authority. Accessed 10 Nov. 2017.

p. 82

241. Ibid.

p. 83

242. Mora, Sherri, and William Ruger. *The State of Texas: Government, Politics, and Policy.* 2nd ed., McGraw Hill Education, 2015, p. 170.

243. Rice, Bradley R. "Commission Form of City Government." *Handbook of Texas Online*, Texas State Historical Association, 12 June 2010, https://www.tshaonline.org/handbook/online/articles/moc01.

244. Ibid.

245. Ibid.

246. Portland, Oregon. "Government: Elected Officials." *City of Portland, Oregon*, https://www.portlandoregon.gov/25783. Accessed 10 Nov. 2017.

p. 84

247. MacCorkle, Stuart A. "Mayor-Council Form of City Government." *Handbook of Texas Online*, Texas State Historical Association, 15 June 2010, https://tshaonline.org/handbook/online/articles/mom01.

248. Ibid.

249. Ibid.

250. Ibid.

251. Mora, Sherri, and William Ruger. *The State of Texas: Government, Politics, and Policy.* 2nd ed., McGraw Hill Education, 2015, p. 170.

252. Blodgett, Terrell Blodgett. "Council-Manager Form of City Government." *Handbook of Texas Online*, Texas State Historical Association, 12 June 2010, https://tshaonline.org/handbook/online/articles/moc02.

253. Ibid.

254. Ibid.

p. 85

255. "Special Districts." *National League of Cities*, www.nlc.org/local-us-governments. Accessed 10 Nov. 2017.

256. "Interim Report to the 82nd Texas Legislature, House Select Committee on Special Purpose Districts." *Texas House of Representatives*, January 2011, p. 31, http://www.house.state.tx.us/_media/pdf/committees/reports/81inte rim/House-Select-Committee-on-Special-Purpose-Districts-Interim-Re

port-2010.pdf.

257. "Brazos River Authority." *Handbook of Texas Online*. Texas State Historical Association, 12 June 2010, http://www.tshaonline.org/handbook/online/articles/mwb01.

258. *Lower Neches Valley Authority*, http://lnva.dst.tx.us/about/. Accessed 10 Nov. 2017.

259. Ibid.

260. "Clean Water for a Healthy Environment," *Trinity River Authority of Texas*, www.trinityra.org. Accessed 10 Nov. 2017.

261. Ibid.

p. 86

262. Ibid.

Chapter 5

p. 89

263. "About the Elections Division." *Texas Secretary of State*, https://www.sos.state.tx.us/elections/index.shtml. Accessed 10 Nov. 2017.

p. 90

264. "County Parties and Chairs." *Texas Secretary of State*, https://www.sos.state.tx.us/elections/index.shtml. Accessed 10 Nov. 2017.

265. "Election Officials and Officeholders." *Texas Secretary of State*, https://www.sos.state.tx.us/elections/voter/current.shtml. Accessed 10 Nov. 2017.

p. 91

266. Ramsey, Ross. "Analysis: Straight-Ticket Voting Could Hobble Swing-District Candidates." *The Texas Tribune*, 10 June 2016, https://www.texastribune.org/2016/06/10/analysis-straight-ticket-voting-could-hobble-swing/.

267. Jacobson, Louis. "The Rise and Simultaneous Fall of Straight-Ticket Voting." *Governing*, eRepublic, 14 July 2016, http://www.governing.com/topics/elections/gov-straight-ticket-voting-states.html.

268. Friedman, Courtney. "Texas House Speaker Wants to End Straight-Ticket Voting." *ABC KSAT-12 News*, Graham Media Group, 1 Feb. 2017, http://www.ksat.com/news/politics/texas-house-speaker-joe-straus-wants-to-end-straight-ticket-voting.

269. McCullough, Jolie. "Gov. Abbott Signs Bill to Eliminate Straight-Ticket Voting Beginning in 2020." *The Texas Tribune*, 1 June 2017, https://www.texastribune.org/2017/06/01/texas-gov-greg-abbott-signs-bill-eliminate-straight-ticket-voting/.

270. Batheja, Aman. "Texas' Shift From Blue to Red Informs 2014 Races." *The Texas Tribune*, 6 June 2014, https://www.texastribune.org/2014/06/06/how-texas-shifted-blue-red-informs-democrats-today/.

p. 93

271. Hansen, Liane, interview with Jesse Sheidlower, editor-at-large, *Oxford English Dictionary*. "A Lobbyist by Another Name?" *National Public Radio*, Weekend Edition Sunday, 22 Jan. 2006, http://www.npr.org/templates/story/story.php?storyId=5167187.

p. 94

272. Smith, Ralph A. "Grange." *Handbook of Texas Online*, Texas State Historical Association, 13 Nov. 2017, https://tshaonline.org/handbook/online/articles/aag01.

273. Ibid.

274. Mora, Sherri, and William Ruger. *The State of Texas: Government, Politics, and Policy*. 2nd ed., McGraw Hill Education, 2014, p. 256.

p. 95

275. May, Janice C. "Texas Legislature." *Handbook of Texas Online*, Texas State Historical Association, 19 July 2017, https://tshaonline.org/handbook/online/articles/mkt02.

276. Young, Nancy Beck. "Democratic Party." *Handbook of Texas Online*, Texas State Historical Association, 12 June 2010, https://tshaonline.org/handbook/online/articles/wad01.

277. Ibid.

p. 96

278. Barnes, Donna A. "People's Party." *Handbook of Texas Online*, Texas State Historical Association, 15 June 2010, https://tshaonline.org/handbook/online/articles/wap01.

279. "Libertarian Party of Texas." *The Texas Tribune* , https://www.texastribune.org/feeds/tribpedia/libertarian-party-of-tex as/. Accessed 13 Nov. 2017.

p. 97

280. Siegel, Stanley E. "A Political History of the Texas Republic, 1836–1845." Dissertation, Rice University, 1953. *Rice Digital Scholarship Archive*, http://hdl.handle.net/1911/18448.

281. Young, Nancy Beck. "Democratic Party." *Handbook of Texas Online*, Texas State Historical Association, 12 June 2010, https://tshaonline.org/handbook/online/articles/wad01.

282. Ibid.

283. Ibid.

284. Ibid.

p. 98

285. "Sam Houston." *Biography*, A&E Television Networks, 7 Nov. 2016, http://www.biography.com/people/sam-houston-9344806.

286. Ibid.

287. Robenalt, Jeffery. "Sam Houston and Mirabeau Lamar: A Contrast of Visions." *Texas Escapes*, 1 May 2012, http://texasescapes.com/JefferyRobenalt/Sam-Houston-and-Mirabea u-Lamar-A-Contrast-of-Visions.htm.

288. "Mirabeau B. Lamar." *Texas State Library and Archives Commission*, 16 Mar. 2016, https://www.tsl.texas.gov/exhibits/presidents/lamar/grow.html.

289. Gambrell, Herbert. "Lamar, Mirabeau Buonaparte." *Handbook of Texas Online*, Texas State Historical Association, 21 Mar. 2016, http://www.tshaonline.org/handbook/online/articles/fla15.

290. Ibid.

291. Robenalt, Jeffery. "Sam Houston and Mirabeau Lamar: A Contrast of Visions." *Texas Escapes*, 1 May 2012, http://texasescapes.com/JefferyRobenalt/Sam-Houston-and-Mirabea u-Lamar-A-Contrast-of-Visions.htm.

p. 99

292. Buenger, Walter L. "Whigs." *Handbook of Texas Online*, Texas State Historical Association, 15 June 2010, https://tshaonline.org/handbook/online/articles/waw01.

293. Buenger, Walter L., and James Alex Baggett. "Constitutional Union Party." *Handbook of Texas Online*, Texas State Historical Association, 12 June 2010, https://tshaonline.org/handbook/online/articles/wac01.

294. "Musings from Sam Houston's Stomping Grounds." *Newton Gresham Library*, Sam Houston State University, Episode 22, 3 Aug. 2007, http://library.shsu.edu/about/podcasts/transcripts/Musings_Houston.pdf.

p. 100

295. "Death of Gen. Sam Houston." *New York Times*, 3 Nov. 1861, www.nytimes.com/1861/11/03/news/death-of-gen-sam-houston.html.

296. "Steamboat House." *Texas Escapes,* www.texasescapes.com/EastTexasTowns/HuntsvilleTexas/Steamboat-House.htm. Accessed 13 Nov. 2017.

297. "Oakwood Cemetery." *Walker County History*, Walker County Historical Commission, www.walkercountyhistory.org/oakwood_cemetery.php. Accessed 13 Nov. 2017.

298. "Musings from Sam Houston's Stomping Grounds." *Newton Gresham Library*, Sam Houston State University, Episode 22, August 3, 2007, http://library.shsu.edu/about/podcasts/transcripts/Musings_Houston.pdf.

p. 101

299. Young, Nancy Beck. "Democratic Party." *Handbook of Texas Online*, Texas State Historical Association, 12 June 2010, https://tshaonline.org/handbook/online/articles/wad01.

300. Young, Nancy Beck. "Democratic Party." *Handbook of Texas Online*, Texas State Historical Association, 12 June 2010, https://tshaonline.org/handbook/online/articles/wad01.

301. Ibid.

302. "Yellow Dog and Blue Dog Democrats." *The Texas Politics Project*, University of Texas at Austin, https://texaspolitics.utexas.edu/archive/html/part/features/0304_01/dogs.html. Accessed 14 Nov. 2017.
303. Ibid.

p. 102
304. Young, Nancy Beck. "Democratic Party." *Handbook of Texas Online*, Texas State Historical Association, 12 June 2010, https://tshaonline.org/handbook/online/articles/wad01.
305. Odintz, Mark. "Yarborough, Ralph Webster." *Handbook of Texas Online*, Texas State Historical Association, 15 June 2010, https://tshaonline.org/handbook/online/articles/fyags.

p. 103
306. Eason, Susan. "Tower, John Goodwin." *Handbook of Texas Online*, Texas State Historical Association, 7 July 2016, https://tshaonline.org/handbook/online/articles/ftoss.
307. Cunningham, Sean P. *Cowboy Conservativism: Texas and the Rise of the Modern Right*. University of Kentucky Press, 2010.
308. Young, Nancy Beck. "Democratic Party." *Handbook of Texas Online*, Texas State Historical Association, 12 June 2010, https://tshaonline.org/handbook/online/articles/wad01.
309. Ibid.
310. *Smith v. Allwright*. 321 U. S. 649. 1944.

p. 104
311. "Voting Rights Act: The Poll Tax." *Marion Butts Collection*, Dallas Public Library, http://dallaslibrary2.org/mbutts/assets/lessons/L9-voting+rights/Marion%20Butts%20-%20Voting%20Rights(PPT).pdf. Accessed 14 Nov. 2017.
312. Ibid.
313. *Harper v. Virginia State Board of Elections*. 383 U. S. 663. 1966.
314. "Collections: Congressman Jack Brooks." *Briscoe Center for American History*, University of Texas at Austin, www.cah.utexas.edu/collections/congress_politics_brooks_bio.php. Accessed 14 Nov. 2017.

p. 105

315. "Presidential Elections and Primaries in Texas, 1848–2012." *Texas Almanac*, Texas State Historical Association, http://texasalmanac.com/topics/elections/presidential-elections-and-primaries-texas-1848-2012. Accessed 14 Nov. 2017.

316. Kinch, Sam, Jr. "Sharpstown Stock-Fraud Scandal." *Handbook of Texas Online*, Texas State Historical Association, 15 June 2010, https://tshaonline.org/handbook/online/articles/mqs01.

317. Young, Nancy Beck. "Democratic Party." *Handbook of Texas Online*, Texas State Historical Association, 12 June 2010, https://tshaonline.org/handbook/online/articles/wad01.

318. Johnson, John G. "Dirty Thirty." *Handbook of Texas Online*, Texas State Historical Association, 12 June 2010, https://tshaonline.org/handbook/online/articles/wmdsh.

319. Sweany, Brian D. "Dirty Thirty." *Texas Monthly*, Sept. 2001, https://www.texasmonthly.com/ politics/dirty-thirty/.

320. Kinch, Sam, Jr. "Sharpstown Stock-Fraud Scandal." *Handbook of Texas Online*, Texas State Historical Association, 15 June 2010, https://tshaonline.org/handbook/online/articles/mqs01.

p. 106

321. Young, Nancy Beck. "Democratic Party." *Handbook of Texas Online*, Texas State Historical Association, 12 June 2010, https://tshaonline.org/handbook/online/articles/wad01.

322. Kinch, Sam, Jr. "Sharpstown Stock-Fraud Scandal." *Handbook of Texas Online*, Texas State Historical Association, 15 June 2010, https://tshaonline.org/handbook/online/articles/mqs01.

323. Slaughter, George. "Clements, William Perry, Jr. [Bill]." *Handbook of Texas Online*, Texas State Historical Association, 26 Oct. 2016, https://tshaonline.org/handbook/online/articles/fcl61.

324. Young, Nancy Beck. "Democratic Party." *Handbook of Texas Online*, Texas State Historical Association, 12 June 2010, https://tshaonline.org/handbook/online/articles/wad01.

325. Elisha Pease and Miriam A. "Ma" Ferguson are the two other governors to serve non-consecutive terms. See: Slaughter, George. "Clements, William Perry, Jr. [Bill]." *Handbook of Texas Online*, Texas State Historical Association, 26 Oct. 2016, https://tshaonline.org/handbook/online/articles/fcl61.

p. 107

326. "Yellow Dog and Blue Dog Democrats." *The Texas Politics Project*, University of Texas at Austin, https://texaspolitics.utexas.edu/archive/html/part/features/0304_01/dogs.html. Accessed 14 Nov. 2017.

327. Suddath, Claire. "A Brief History of Blue Dog Democrats." *Time*, 28 July 2009, http://content.time.com/time/politics/article/0,8599,1913057,00.html.

328. McCaleb, Ian Christopher. "GOP Budget Hawk Gramm Won't Seek Re-election." *Inside Politics*, Cable News Network, 5 Sept. 2001, www.cnn.com/2001/ALLPOLITICS/09/04/gramm.senate/index.html.

329. King, Wayne. "Texas Conservative Defeats Rival for Senate Seat Tower Gave Up." *New York Times*, 7 Nov. 1984, www.nytimes.com/1984/11/07/us/texas-conservative-defeats-rival-for-senate-seat-tower-gave-up.html.

330. Young, Nancy Beck. "Democratic Party." *Handbook of Texas Online*, Texas State Historical Association, 12 June 2010, https://tshaonline.org/handbook/online/articles/wad01.

331. Moneyhon, Carl H. "Republican Party." *Handbook of Texas Online*, Texas State Historical Association, 15 June 2010, https://tshaonline.org/handbook/online/articles/war02.

332. Moneyhon, Carl H. "Republican Party," *Handbook of Texas Online*, Texas State Historical Association, 15 June 2010, https://tshaonline.org/handbook/online/articles/war02.

p. 108

333. "Texas Politics: Political Parties." *Liberal Arts Technology Instructional Services*, University of Texas at Austin, www.laits.utexas.edu/txp_media/html/part/print_part.html. Accessed 14 Nov. 2017.

334. McNeely, Dave. "DeLay, Cronies Hurt Texas in U.S. House." *The Victoria Advocate*, NewsBank, 4 Dec. 2006, http://infoweb.newsbank.com/resources/doc/nb/news/115C52052E3 0BCD0?p=NewsBank.

p. 109

335. Tilove, Jonathan. "Greg Abbott: The Calm after the Rick Perry

Storm." *my Statesman: from Austin American-Statesman*, Cox Media Group, 20 June 2015, http://www.mystatesman.com/news/state-regional-govt-politics/greg-abbott-the-calm-after-the-rick-perry-storm/saoq3hkRQaZHIurdsNImaN/.

336. Perry, Rick. "Rick Perry: Follow the Texas Model of Success." *USA Today*, 28 Oct. 2013, https://www.usatoday.com/story/opinion/2013/10/28/governor-rick-perry-texas-tour-jobs-editorials-debates/3290927/.

p. 110

337. Krauss, Clifford, and Nelson D. Schwartz. "Rick Perry Hones His Image as 'Texas Miracle' Fades." *New York Times*, 3 June 2015, https://www.nytimes.com/2015/06/04/business/economy/what-texas-economy-means-for-rick-perrys-presidential-ambitions.html?_r=0.

338. Ibid.

339. Ibid.

340. Mooney, Chris. "Oil Prices Keep Falling—This Is Why." *The Washington Post*, 21 Dec. 2015, https://www.washingtonpost.com/news/energy-environment/wp/2015/12/21/oil-prices-keep-falling-this-is-the-reason-why/?utm_term=.7b55cb9d1ec9.

341. Ibid.

342. Domm, Patti. "The Drillers of West Texas Are Ready to Undermine any OPEC, Russia Deal to Boost Oil Prices." *CNBC*, 16 May 2017, https://www.cnbc.com/2017/05/16/the-drillers-of-west-texas-are-ready-to-undermine-any-opec-russia-deal-to-boost-oil-prices.html.

343. "The Shale Gas and Tight Oil Boom: U.S. States' Economic Gains and Vulnerabilities." *Council on Foreign Relations*, 15 Oct. 2013, https://www.cfr.org/report/shale-gas-and-tight-oil-boom.

344. Deam, Jenny. "Texas Uninsured Rate Falls to 16.8%; National Rate Now in Single Digits." *Houston Chronicle*, Hearst Newspapers, 17 May 2016, www.houstonchronicle.com/business/medical/article/Texas-uninsured-rate-falls-to-16-8-national-7542199.php; also CDC in same source.

345. Ehrenfreund, Max. "The Facts about Rick Perry and the 'Texas Miracle.'" *Wonkblog*, The Washington Post, 8 June 2015, https://www.washingtonpost.com/news/wonk/wp/2015/06/08/the-fa

cts-about-rick-
perry-and-the-texas-miracle/?utm_term=.6f120478a763

p. 111
346. Mann, Dave. "Party Hopping." *Texas Monthly*, May 2017,
https://www.texasmonthly.com/politics/party-hopping/.
347. Chris Wallace, quoted in:
Ramsey, Ross. "Analysis: A Bathroom Mess for Republican Texas
Lawmakers." *Texas Tribune*, 7 Dec. 2016,
https://www.texastribune.org/2016/12/07/analysis-bathroom-mess-re
publican-texas-lawmakers/.
348. Mann, Dave. "Party Hopping." *Texas Monthly*, May 2017,
https://www.texasmonthly.com/politics/party-hopping/.
349. *Roe v. Wade*. 410 U.S. 113. 1973.
350. *Planned Parenthood v. Casey*. 505 U.S. 833. 1992.

p. 112
351. Swartz, Mimi. "Mothers, Sisters, Daughters, Wives." *Texas
Monthly*, Aug. 2012,
https://www.texasmonthly.com/politics/mothers-sisters-daughters-wi
ves/.
352. Ibid.
353. Sid Miller, quoted in:
Swartz, Mimi. "Mothers, Sisters, Daughters, Wives." *Texas Monthly*,
Aug. 2012,
https://www.texasmonthly.com/politics/mothers-sisters-daughters-wi
ves/.
354. Swartz, Mimi. "Mothers, Sisters, Daughters, Wives." *Texas
Monthly*, Aug. 2012,
https://www.texasmonthly.com/politics/mothers-sisters-daughters-wi
ves/.
355. Luthra, Shefali. "Perry Signs Omnibus Abortion Bill Into Law."
The Texas Tribune, 18 July 2013,
https://www.texastribune.org/2013/07/18/perry-signs-abortion-bill-la
w/.
356. Ibid.
357. Ibid.
358. Haynes, Danielle. "Appeals Court Upholds Strict Texas Abortion

Law Closing All but Seven Clinics." *UPI*, 9 June 2015, https://www.upi.com/Top_News/US/2015/06/09/Appeals-court-uph olds-strict-Texas-abortion-law-closing-all-but-seven-clinics/278143387 4032/.

359. Novack, Sophie. "Austin Abortion Clinic Reopens after Supreme Court Ruling. Will Any More Follow?" *Texas Observer*, 25 Apr. 2017, https://www.texasobserver.org/texas-abortion-clinic-reopens-supreme -court-ruling-will-any-more-follow/.

360. Ibid.

361. Associated Press. "Austin Abortion Clinic Reopens Following High Court Ruling." *U.S. News and World Report*, 28 Apr. 2017, https://www.usnews.com/news/best-states/texas/articles/2017-04-28 /austin-abortion-clinic-reopens-following-high-court-ruling.

362. Pestano, Andrew V. "Planned Parenthood Reopens First Abortion Clinic in Texas." *UPI*, 3 May 2017, https://www.upi.com/Top_News/US/2017/05/03/Planned-Parenthoo d-reopens-first-abortion-clinic-in-Texas/9171493809984/.

363. *District of Columbia v. Heller*. 554 U.S. 570. 2008.

364. *McDonald v. Chicago*. 561 U. S. 742. 2010.

p. 113

365. *Barron v. Baltimore*. 32 U.S. 243. 1833.

366. "Right to Keep and Bear Arms." *Texas Constitution* (1876). Article 1, Section 23.

367. McGaughy, Lauren. "First to Ban Open Carry, Texas Could Be One of the Last to OK It." *Houston Chronicle*, 22 Dec. 2014, www.houstonchronicle.com/news/politics/texas/article/First-to-ban-o pen-carry-Texas-could-be-one-of-5974401.php.

368. Ibid.

369. Butterfield, Fox. "ON THE RECORD: Governor Bush on Crime; Bush's Law and Order Adds Up to Tough and Popular." *The New York Times*, 18 Aug. 1999, www.nytimes.com/1999/08/18/us/record-governor-bush-crime-bush- s-law-order-adds-up-tough-popular.html.

370. Ibid.

371. Watkins, Matthew. "Campus Carry Opponents Wage New Battle Before Law Takes Effect." *The Texas Tribune*, 1 Oct. 2015, https://www.texastribune.org/2015/10/01/schools-consider-gun-rules

-campus-carry-opponents-/.

372. Ibid.

373. Costa-Roberts, Daniel. "Texas Approves Open Carry Law for Handguns." *PBS*, PBS Newshour, 30 May 2015, https://www.pbs.org/newshour/rundown/texas-verge-passing-open-carry-law/.

374. Aguilar, Julián. "At Shooting Range, Abbott Signs 'Open Carry' Bill." *The Texas Tribune*, 13 June 2015, https://www.texastribune.org/2015/06/13/abbott-signs-open-carry-bill/.

p. 114

375. "Texas Gun Fees Now Nation's Lowest with New Law." *Beaumont Enterprise*, Hearst Newspapers, 26 May 2017, www.beaumontenterprise.com/news/article/Texas-gun-fees-now-nation-s-lowest-with-new-law-11176853.php.

376. C. J. Grisham, quoted in:
Parker, Kolten. "NRA Blasts Open Carry Texas after San Antonio Incidents." *mySA*, Hearst Newspapers, 2 June 2014, www.mysanantonio.com/news/local/article/NRA-blasts-Open-Carry-Texas-after-San-Antonio-5522959.php.

377. Parker, Kolten. "NRA Blasts Open Carry Texas after San Antonio Incidents." *mySA*, Hearst Newspapers, 2 June 2014, www.mysanantonio.com/news/local/article/NRA-blasts-Open-Carry-Texas-after-San-Antonio-5522959.php.

378. Ibid.

379. National Rifle Association. "NRA-ILA's Chris Cox Talks About Open Carry and Failure of Gun Control in CA." *YouTube*, 3 June 2014, https://www.youtube.com/watch?v=m2GThvEXDUY&feaature=share.

380. Boerma, Lindsey. "NRA Official: Shaming Open-carry Texas Gun Groups Was 'a Mistake.'" *CBS News*, 4 June 2014, https://www.cbsnews.com/news/nra-official-shaming-open-carry-texas-gun-groups-was-a-mistake/.

381. Grieder, Erica. "Pistol Pushers." *Texas Monthly*, April 2015, https://www.texasmonthly.com/politics/pistol-pushers/.

382. Parker, Kolten. "NRA blasts Open Carry Texas after San Antonio Incidents," *mySA*, Hearst Newspapers, 2 June 2014, https://www.mysanantonio.com/news/local/article/NRA-blasts-Open-

Carry-Texas-after-San-Antonio-5522959.php.

383. Aguilar, Julian. "At Shooting Range, Abbott Signs 'Open Carry' Bill." *The Texas Tribune*, 13 June 2015, https://www.texastribune.org/2015/06/13/abbott-signs-open-carry-bill/.

384. Lindell, Chuck. "License-free Gun Bills Draw Capitol Crowd." *myStatesman: from Austin American-Statesman*, Cox Media Group, 28 Mar. 2017, www.mystatesman.com/news/license-free-gun-bills-draw-capitol-crowd/4xQyNBdFzFMwoBt9vFWAXM/.

385. Grisham, C. J., quoted in:
Chuck Lindell. "License-free Gun Bills Draw Capitol Crowd." *myStatesman: from Austin American-Statesman*, Cox Media Group, 28 Mar. 2017, www.mystatesman.com/news/license-free-gun-bills-draw-capitol-crowd/4xQyNBdFXzFMwoBt9vFWAXM/.

p. 115
386. "Race Summary Report: 2016 General Election: 11/8/2016." *Office of the Secretary of State*, http://elections.sos.state.tx.us/elchist319_state.htm. Accessed 14 Nov. 2017.

387. Ramsey, Ross. "Analysis: The Blue Dots in Texas' Red Political Sea." *The Texas Tribune*, 11 Nov. 2016, https://www.texastribune.org/2016/11/11/analysis-blue-dots-texas-red-political-sea/.

388. Ibid.

389. "Race Summary Report: 2016 General Election: 11/8/2016." *Office of the Secretary of State*, http://elections.sos.state.tx.us/elchist319_state.htm. Accessed 14 Nov. 2017.

p. 116
390. Greider, Erica. "Pistol Pushers." *Texas Monthly*, April 2015, https://www.texasmonthly.com politics/pistol-pushers/.

391. Ibid.

Unit 3
Chapter 6
p. 124
392. Huddleston, John D. Huddleston. "Ferguson, Miriam Amanda Wallace (Ma)." *The Handbook of Texas*, Texas State Historical Association, 21 Jan. 2017, https://tshaonline.org/handbook/online/articles/ffe06.
393. Ibid.

p. 125
394. Green, George N. "O'Daniel, Wilbert Lee (Pappy)." *Handbook of Texas Online*, Texas State Historical Association, 22 Feb. 2016, https://tshaonline.org/handbook/online/articles/fod11.

p. 127
395. Ura, Alexa, and Jolie McCullough. "Once Again, the Texas Legislature is Mostly White, Male, Middle-aged." *The Texas Tribune*, 9 Jan. 2017, https://www.texastribune.org/2017/01/09/texas-legislature-mostly-white-male-middle-aged/.
396. Research Division of the Texas Legislative Council. "The Legislative Process in Texas." *Texas Legislative Council for 85th Legislature*, Nov. 2016, p. 2, www.tlc.texas.gov/docs/legref/legislativeprocess.pdf.
397. Ibid., p. 3.

p.128
398. "How a Bill Becomes a Law." *Texas House of Representatives*, www.house.state.tx.us/about-us/bill/. Accessed 15 Nov. 2017.
399. Ibid.

p. 129
400. "How a Bill Becomes a Law." *Texas House of Representatives*, www.house.state.tx.us.about-us/bill/. Accessed 15 Nov. 2017.
401. "How a Bill Becomes a Law." *Texas House of Representatives*, www.house.state.tx.us/about-us/bill/. Accessed 15 Nov. 2017.

p.131
402. "Citizen Handbook: How the State Legislature Works." *Texas Senate*, Feb. 2015, p. 12, www.senate.texas.gov/_assets/pdf/Citizen_HBook_Web_2015.pdf.

Chapter 7
p. 134
403. *Clinton v. City of New York.* 524 U. S. 417. 1998.

p. 138
404. *Texas Constitution*, Article 15, Sect. 8. *Texas Constitution and Statutes*, 4 Nov. 1980, www.statutes.legis.state.tx.us/Docs/CN/htm/CN.15.htm#15.8.

p. 139
405. "Amendments to the Texas Constitution Since 1876: Current through the November 3, 2015, Constitutional Amendment Election." *Texas Legislative Council*, Feb. 2016, p. 50, www.tlc.state.tx.us/docs/amendments/Constamend1876.pdf.
406. William Clements was elected to two four-year terms as governor (1978 and 1986), but his terms were not consecutive.
407. "Amendments to the Texas Constitution Since 1876: Current through the November 3, 2015, Constitutional Amendment Election." *Texas Legislative Council*, Feb. 2016, p. 49, www.tlc.state.tx.us/docs/amendments/Constamend1876.pdf.
408. Ibid.

p. 140
409. "Land and Land Management." *The Texas General Land Office*, www.glo.texas.gov/land/land-management/overview/index.html. Accessed 16 Nov. 2017.
410. Ibid.
411. Ibid.

p. 141
412. "What Does the Texas Department of Agriculture (TDA) do?" *Texas Department of Agriculture*, www.texasagriculture.gov/About/WhatdoesTDAdo.aspx. Accessed 16

Nov. 2017.

413. Ibid.

414. Smith, Morgan. "In Private Meeting, [Agriculture Commissioner] Sid Miller Says Hog Poison Safeguard Is Not 'Doable.'" *The Texas Tribune*, 15 May 2017, https://www.texastribune.org/2017/05/15/private-meeting-sid-miller-says-hog-poison-restrictions-not-doable/.

415. "Duties and Responsibilities of the Office of the Attorney General." *The Attorney General of Texas*, https://www.texasattorneygeneral.gov/agency/duties-responsibilities-of-the-office-of-the-attorney-general. Accessed 16 Nov. 2017.

416. "Constitutional Duties." *Texas Secretary of State*, https://www.sos.state.tx.us/about/duties.shtml. Accessed 16 Nov. 2017.

417. Ibid.

p. 142

418. Ibid.

419. A list of the state agencies, boards, and commissions can be found at:
Texas State Directory, https://www.txdirectory.com/online/abc/.

420. "SBOE—State Board of Education." *Texas Education Agency*, https://tea.texas.gov/sboe/. Accessed 16 Nov. 2017.

421. "Texas State Board of Education." *Texas State Library and Archives Commission*, www.lib.utexas.edu/taro/tslac/30140/tsl-30140.html. Accessed 16 Nov. 2017.

422. "Texas Board of Criminal Justice: Overview." *Texas Department of Criminal Justice*, https://www.tdcj.state.tx.us/tbcj/index.html. Accessed 16 Nov. 2017.

p. 143

423. "The Organization." *Texas Alcoholic Beverage Commission*, 26 Apr. 2017, www.tabc.state.tx.us/about_us/the_organization.asp.

Chapter 8

p. 146

424. Additional federal intermediate courts such as the Court of

Military Appeals and the Court of Appeals for the Federal Circuit also exist, as well as additional lower courts including the U. S. Court of International Trade, U.S. Tax Court, and the Court of Veterans Appeals.

p. 149
425. *Fletcher v. Peck.* 10 U.S. 87. 1810.
426. *Furman v. Georgia.* 408 U.S. 238. 1972.
427. *Gregg v. Georgia.* 428 U.S. 153. 1976.

p. 150
428. "States with and without the Death Penalty." 9 Nov. 2016, *Death Penalty Information Center*,
https://deathpenaltyinfo.org/states-and-without-death-penalty.
429. "Death Sentences in the United States from 1977 by State and Year." *Death Penalty Information Center*, 2016,
https://deathpenaltyinfo.org/death-sentences-united-states-1977-present.
430. "Number of Executions by State and Region Since 1976." *Death Penalty Information Center*, 9 Nov. 2017,
https://deathpenaltyinfo.org/number-executions-state-and-region-1976.

p. 151
431. *Ford v. Wainwright.* 477 U. S. 399. 1986.
432. *Atkins v. Virginia.* 536 U. S. 304. 2002.
433. *Roper v. Simmons.* 543 U. S. 551. 2005.
434. Walpin, Ned. "Why is Texas #1 in Executions?" *Frontline*, PBS/Houston Public Media,
www.pbs.org/wgbh/pages/frontline/shows/execution/readings/texas.html. Accessed 16 Nov. 2017.
435. Ibid.
436. Ramsey, Ross. "UT/TT Poll: Texans Stand behind Death Penalty." 24 May 2012, *The Texas Tribune*,
https://www.texastribune.org/2012/05/24/uttt-poll-life-and-death/.

p. 152
437. *Brown v. Board of Education of Topeka, Kansas.* 347 U.S. 483. 1954.

438. *Reed v. Reed.* 404 U.S. 71. 1971.
439. Nicholson, Eric. "Texas Falls out of Love with the Death Penalty, Embraces Life without Parole." 17 Dec. 2015, *Dallas Observer*, www.dallasobserver.com/news/texas-falls-out-of-love-with-the-death-penalty-embraces-life-without-parole-7860819.
440. Ibid.

p. 154
441. "About Texas Courts." *Texas Judicial Branch*, www.txcourts.gov/about-texas-courts/courts-of-appeals.aspx. Accessed 16 Nov. 2017.

p. 155
442. "Texas County Officials." *Texas Association of Counties*, https://www.county.org/texas-county-government/texas-county-offici als/Pages/default.aspx. Accessed 16 Nov. 2017.
443. Ibid.
444. Womack, Paul. "Judiciary." *Handbook of Texas Online*, Texas State Historical Association, 15 June 2010. https://tshaonline.org/handbook/online/articles/jzj01.
445. "Texas County Commissioner." *Texas Association of Counties*, https://www.county.org/texas-county-government/texas-county-offici als/Pages/County-Commissioner.aspx. Accessed 16 Nov. 2017.

p. 156
446. Womack, Paul. "Judiciary." *Handbook of Texas Online*, Texas State Historical Association, 15 June 2010, https://tshaonline.org/handbook/online/articles/jzj01.
447. "Texas County Commissioner." *Texas Association of Counties*, https://www.county.org/texas-county-government/texas-county-offici als/Pages/County-Commissioner.aspx. Accessed 16 Nov. 2017.
448. "About Texas Courts." *Texas Judicial Branch*, www.txcourts.gov/about-texas-courts/trial-courts/. Accessed 16 Nov. 2017.
449. Ibid.
450. Ibid.

p. 157
451. Ibid.
452. Ibid.
453. Ibid.

i. Lyman, Rick. "Bob Bullock, a Titan of Texas Politics, Is Dead at 69."
New York Times, 19 June 1999,
http://www.nytimes.com/1999/06/19/us/bob-bullock-a-titan-of-texas
-politics-is-dead-at-69.html.